What others are saying about **Where's the Map?**

"What a GREAT gift for a young person! What a 'dream' book for them to create and guide their own future! It is excellent and I will definitely encourage my students to spend thoughtful time with it as they begin their work with me. You present so many levels and layers of options and possibilities for young people, which they rarely have the opportunity to see, let alone explore in their school-structured lives. There can be a great deal of anxiety and tension around being 16-18 . . . 'life' is coming at young people so rapidly and they feel their capabilities and their weaknesses acutely. Your book could provide the antidote to that tension—a personal and private opportunity to examine, honor, and indeed celebrate the unique potential of every young person willing to take a good close look at her or his 'self'."

> **Joyce Reed**, Former Associate Dean of the College at Brown University
> Nationally recognized expert in student mentoring and advising
> **www.collegegoals.com**

"*Where's the Map?* is a helpful guide for anyone wanting to identify, explore and clarify their personal and professional life goals, hopes and dreams. Readers will find the "roadmaps" provide valuable help in self exploration of "what's next" for determining and working toward whatever the future holds! The tools and information provided are concrete and easy to follow and implement. A great resource for high school students, college students, graduates, adults searching for a change, and educators."

> **Michelle W. Legault,** Outreach Counselor for first-generation college bound students

"My first response to *Where's the Map?* was "I should be recommending this to every gap year student with whom I am working!" It is a wonderfully clear and practical guidebook for introspection and planned action. Although geared toward post graduates, *Where's the Map?* could be utilized by older adults as well. Most people, myself included, could use a workbook like this to clarify interests and goals. And then make them happen."

> **Holly Bull**, President for Center for Interim Programs, LLC
> **www.interimprograms.com**

Continued from front cover: "This marvelous book is for anyone who refuses to settle for the lackluster, mediocre existence that quietly takes over most people's lives. You can settle, or you can figure out the life you want to live, and go for it. With its revealing questions and thought-provoking exercises, *Where's the Map?* will help you draw your own map for getting there."

> **John Goddard**, Author of *The Survivor: 24 Spine-Chilling Adventures on the Edge of Death*
> **www.johngoddard.info**

"WOW! Jim and Beth have provided a BRILLIANT guiding light for today's youth who are eager to figure out where and how they want to spend their tomorrows. *Where's the Map?* offers serious help in a playful, fun manner - making it a great gift for anyone transitioning from adolescence into adulthood. In fact, I've just given this book to my oldest daughter who is about to take a "gap year" away from college, and I can't thank the Hoods enough for this timely resource!"

> **Dr. Peter Montminy**, Child Psychologist, Father of Four
> Director of MidStep Centers for Child Development
> **www.midstep.com**

"Where was this resource when I was young? I wish someone had handed me a copy when I was seventeen. It could have saved me, literally, years of floundering and untold dollars spent. It would have provided awareness and confirmation of my deepest dreams at a crucial time of development."

> **Lynne Hadley**, M.Ed., business and life coach for 20 years
> Lifeworks Coaching and Consulting
> **www.lynnehadley.com**

"This book is something I would definitely take advantage of—it is something all students can relate too. I wish I had something like this for my senior year that explained all the different options for what you can do after high school."

Samantha Goudreau, Sophomore at the University of Vermont

"*Where's the Map?* is a must-have for everyone who wants to live a happy and fulfilling life, which we all do! Beth and Jim not only live what they teach, but they have organized the information in such a way that it makes sense for everyone, no matter if you are a recent college grad, someone whose map flew out the window mid-trip, or if you forgot to get one in the first place! Living by your values is so basic, yet somehow so difficult to conceptualize without a guide to help. This guide will help you create the map of the life you want, and help you avoid the pitfalls of living outside of what you believe. I highly recommend this book for everyone— the happiness of your journey depends on it!"

Drew Rabidoux, Licensed Master Social Worker and Life Coach

"Jim told me that he had the idea for this book while we were meditating silently together at sunset on the beach here in Hawaii. That's what I love about Jim and Beth! They live their conviction that our best guidance comes from within. And as a result they have created a magnificent Life Guide that masterfully encourages young people to nurture and balance their fledgeling inner "knowing" with a beautifully articulated set of self-explorations. Jim and Beth are among the very most positive, encouraging and inspiring people I know. Their book will be of immense help to many, many young people! I recommend *Where's the Map?* with delight."

Dr. Michael Aronowitz, Licensed Psychologist

"The inspiring readings and activities in *Where's the Map?* make it simple for each individual to gather their thoughts, hone in on their aspirations, and move forward onto the next step of their lives."

Mike Quinlan, Administrative Coordinator, LEAPNOW: Transforming Education
www.leapnow.org

"*Where's the Map?* helps students to sort out all their options and make decisions they can live with, whether it's to continue education, take some time off, or begin a career they can truly love. Beth and Jim don't make you follow their path; they help you discover your own!"

John Kremer, curator, The College Drop-Out Hall of Fame
www.collegedropouthalloffame.com

"Take the question of what you want to do with the rest of your life seriously. It doesn't matter whether you're still in school or have already finished, whether you're looking at college, jobs, or where to live, *Where's the Map?* will take you though the questions you need to ask yourself before you embark on those big, life-altering decisions."

Penelope Trunk, Author of *The Brazen Careerist: The NEW rules for SUCCESS*
www.penelopetrunk.com

"AWESOME! What a fabulous resource. Not all of us can be so lucky to have Beth and Jim in person for life's important decisions. If I hadn't had the privilege of having them help me along through so many important life milestones and decisions, I would have been happy to have this book! I really like the mission and vision portions of each chapter of life. It is so important to make and keep goals so that there is something that is pushing you to continually reach for your dreams. This book helps people ask themselves the hard life questions, and ground themselves so that they can really be able to achieve their goals. Great!"

Shannon Maureen Hickey, 5th grade English International teacher, American School of Puebla, Mexico
Current Masters student in Administration of Educational Organizations

Where's the Map?™

Create Your OWN Guide
to Life after Graduation

Beth and James Hood

Inspiration Publications, Inc.
Hawaii

Where's the Map?™ Create Your OWN Guide to Life after Graduation
Beth and James Hood

Inspiration Publications, Inc.
Post Office Box 1004
Kamuela HI 96743
808-430-3406
Toll-free Fax:866-535-5167
orders@wheresthemap.com
www.wheresthemap.com

This book includes information from many sources and gathered from many personal experiences. It is published for general reference and is not intended to be a substitute for independent verification by readers when necessary and appropriate. The book is sold with the understanding that neither the authors nor the publisher is engaged in rendering any legal, psychological or career advice. The publisher and author disclaim any personal liability, directly or indirectly, for advice or information presented within. Although the author and publisher have prepared this manuscript with utmost diligent care and have made every effort to ensure the accuracy and completeness of the information contained within, we assume no responsibility for errors, inaccuracies, omissions or inconsistencies.

Printed in the United States of America

10 9 8 7 6 5 4 3 2 1

Publisher's Cataloging-in-Publication
(Provided by Quality Books, Inc.)

    Hood, Beth.
      Where's the map? : create your own guide to life
    after graduation / by Beth and James Hood.
      p. cm.
      LCCN 2008921973
      ISBN-13: 978-0-9799262-0-4
      ISBN-10: 0-9799262-0-3

      1. Young adults--Life skills guides. 2. Young adults
    --Vocational guidance.   I. Hood, James, 1976-
    II. Title.

    HQ799.5.H66 2008   646.7'0084'2
                            QBI08-600055

ATTN: QUANTITY DISCOUNTS ARE AVAILABLE TO YOUR COMPANY, EDUCATIONAL INSTITUTION OR ORGANIZATION for reselling, educational purposes, subscription incentives, gifts or fundraising campaigns.

For more information, please contact the publisher at
Inspiration Publications, Inc., Post Office Box 1004, Kamuela HI 96743
808/430-3406 - orders@wheresthemap.com

Dedication

To John Goddard,
the ultimate
goal-setter and goal-achiever.

Thanks for your inspiration.

Set a goal to see what it will
make of you to achieve it.

—Earl Shoaff

About the Authors

Beth and Jim met in Seattle, while building a house with Habitat for Humanity, and it didn't take them long to realize that they shared a vision. Like most young people, they wanted to live the life of their dreams, but for them, a big part of that dream was to help others discover, live, and breathe their own dreams. Using their educational backgrounds, life experience, and the knowledge gleaned from years of working with high school and college students, they developed a system of exercises that helped them map out the life of their dreams. In *Where's the Map?™ Create Your Own Guide to Life after Graduation*, they share these exercises so that you will be able to answer the question "What do you want to be when you grow up?" a lot sooner than they did—and with a lot fewer false starts.

Beth and Jim live on the Big Island of Hawaii, where they spend most of their time writing and researching. Besides writing and conducting training workshops, the life of their dreams leaves room for diving and snorkeling, kayaking, hikes along the coast, and tropical sunsets.

Special Mahalos

Our sincere thanks to all of our friends and family who have tolerated, supported, encouraged, or prodded us along the way to living the life of our dreams. We know it must have been painful at times to watch us go through so many different types of schooling, careers, long-distance moves, and continuous evolution in our plans. Thank you for your patience and your love. Special thanks to our parents, and to Dr. Chieko Maekawa, for your encouragement to spread our wings.

We'd also like to thank everyone who contributed to our book launch, including, but not limited to:

- Michael Carr, our positively brilliant and insightful editor.
- Seth Andrews and the gang at Fulgen Technology for our web site.
- Steve and Bill Harrison, and the entire Quantum Leap staff, as well as class #5 for your ideas, support, and encouragement.
- Dan Poynter, Peter Bowerman and John Kremer for all the advice and resources you provided about publishing.

Contents

Part 3 — Roadblocks and Detours

Part 4 — Putting It All Together

Part 1

Getting Started

Life Isn't About
Finding Yourself.

It's About
Creating Yourself.

-Unknown

Hey, there,

We're glad you made it to the first page. Since you've come this far, here are a few things we want to share with you:

#1: This is not your typical guidebook.

We aren't here to tell you what to do. In fact, we don't even want you to listen to us!

We want you to listen to yourself.

#2: This book, like your life, will be written by YOU.

Sure, we throw in our two cents here and there, because sometimes it's beneficial to have an outside perspective to help you see things in a new way. In future editions, we want your stories and ideas about life to replace ours.

Ultimately, you call the shots. You make the decisions. YOU fill in the gaps.

#3: Your experience in this world is unique.

Even those who think they know you really well can't completely understand your perspective, because they haven't lived your unique life. Your skills, interests, goals, and dreams are specific to you alone.

That's why your guidebook to life, is not like anyone else's.

Up to this point, your path has been very well defined. You've spent a LOT of your life with teachers, family, and friends telling you where to go and what to do. Now that you're graduating, you might be asking:

"Where's the map showing me where to go next?"

#4: The map to the life of your dreams is inside of you. (What did you think?) We don't expect you to know at this point exactly how you want to live the rest of your life. But you know more than you are letting on. The first step in uncovering this map is to ask yourself a few questions:

• *What do I value most in my life?*
By taking a good look at your values and preferences, you can begin to create your life intentionally, regardless of how clear or foggy your vision is right now.

• *What are my hopes for the future?*
Yes, everybody's got 'em—only sometimes you have to dig a little to find them. This is the place to write down any hopes or dreams for the future, whatever they are. Writing them out gives them more power than holding them inside.

• *What do I need to accomplish my dreams?*
The sooner you can get clear about what you want to do with your life, the sooner you can share your vision with others and create a network of people to support your dreams.

#5: There are unlimited opportunities available for you.
Your options are limited only by what you believe is possible. Your imagination guides your vision for the future.

#6: Take all the time you need.
Don't let anyone tell you that you don't have time to think about what you really want to do with your life. There is always enough time to make these important decisions.

So...Let's get started in creating the map to the rest of your amazing life.

Aloha,
Beth and Jim

Rules of the Road

The point of this book is to provide you with a place to get creative about your life. This is your space to brainstorm what's coming up in the future. So far, you may have been on autopilot, just sort of going through the motions as you went through school. Now is your chance to find your answers to the questions on the sign. You don't need to figure it all out this week or even this year, but this guide will give you a chance to start asking yourself the questions that will shape your life.

There are eight chapters, each designed to help you answer one of these questions. We'd suggest you start with chapter 1, because it lays the framework for the rest of the book. But after that, you don't have to do the chapters in any particular order. If there's a chapter that really jumps out at you, start there.

 If you get stuck during any of the exercises, check out roadblocks and detours in chapter 8. This chapter has some suggestions to help you when you feel as though something is blocking you from pursuing your dreams.

You can also visit **WheresTheMap.com** for more links and helpful ideas.

 Along the way, there are places where you can stop and create a picture of your future. This is your chance to get creative and imagine where you would like to be at these points in the future.

5 Years
10 Years
30 Years
50 Years
End of Life

 When we have a story to share, we'll use these tags to let you know who is talking.

Also, along the way we'll use this icon if we have an example of our own to illustrate how the activity works, and to give you some ideas.

Chapter 1:
What matters to me most?

Chapter 2:
What do you want to know?

Chapter 3:
Need some time to sort all of this out?

Chapter 4:
How do you want to make a living?

Chapter 5:
Where in the world do you fit in?

Chapter 6:
Who do you want to spend your life with?

Chapter 7:
What keeps you going?

Chapter 8:
What's stopping you from living the life of your dreams?

Before you get started, take a look at the next few pages...

Living Life by Design

You may have given up on your childhood dreams, but here's an amazing story about someone who never did. At age five, when John Goddard's uncle asked him what he wanted to be when he grew up, he immediately answered, "Explorer!"

On a rainy afternoon, when he was fifteen, John Goddard sat at the kitchen table with a yellow notepad and made a list of 127 goals, which he called "My Life List." Among other things, it included mountains he wanted to climb, rivers he hoped to explore, and world cultures he intended to study. Since then, he has accomplished 113 of these original goals and has expanded the list to include over 400 more! John never gave up on his dreams. Instead, he turned his dreams into goals, his goals into plans, and his plans into an amazing life. Below is John's Life List. The checked items are all the things he has accomplished.

John Goddard's Life List

EXPLORE:
- ☑ Nile River
- ☑ Amazon River
- ☑ Congo River
- ☑ Colorado River
- ☑ Yangtze River, China
- ❑ Niger River
- ❑ Orinoco River, Venezuela
- ☑ Rio Coco, Nicaragua

STUDY PRIMITIVE CULTURES IN:
- ☑ The Congo
- ☑ New Guinea
- ☑ Brazil
- ☑ Borneo
- ☑ The Sudan
- ☑ Australia
- ☑ Kenya
- ☑ The Philippines
- ☑ Tanganyika (Now Tanzania)
- ☑ Ethiopia
- ☑ Nigeria
- ☑ Alaska

PHOTOGRAPH:
- ☑ Iguaçu Falls, Brazil
- ☑ Victoria Falls, Rhodesia
- ☑ Sutherland Falls, New Zealand
- ☑ Yosemite Falls
- ☑ Niagara Falls
- ☑ Retrace travels of Marco Polo and Alexander the Great

CLIMB:
- ❑ Mt. Everest
- ❑ Mt. Aconcagua, Argentina
- ❑ Mt. McKinley
- ☑ Mt. Hauscarán, Peru
- ☑ Mt. Kilimanjaro
- ☑ Mt. Ararat, Turkey
- ☑ Mt. Kenya
- ❑ Mt. Cook, New Zealand
- ☑ Mt. Popocatepetl, Mexico
- ☑ The Matterhorn
- ☑ Mt. Rainier
- ☑ Mt. Fuji
- ☑ Mt. Vesuvius
- ☑ Mt. Bromo, Java
- ☑ Grand Tetons
- ☑ Mt. Baldy, California

SWIM IN:
- ☑ Lake Victoria
- ☑ Lake Superior
- ☑ Lake Tanganyika
- ☑ Lake Titicaca, S. America
- ☑ Lake Nicaragua

EXPLORE UNDERWATER:
- ☑ Coral reefs of Florida
- ☑ Great Barrier Reef, Australia
- ☑ Red Sea
- ☑ Fiji Islands
- ☑ The Bahamas
- ☑ Explore Okefenokee Swamp and the Everglades

VISIT:

- ☐ North and South Poles
- ☑ Great Wall of China
- ☑ Panama and Suez Canals
- ☑ Easter Island
- ☑ The Galapagos Islands
- ☑ Vatican City (saw the Pope)
- ☑ The Taj Mahal
- ☑ The Eiffel Tower
- ☑ The Blue Grotto
- ☑ The Tower of London
- ☑ The Leaning Tower of Pisa
- ☑ The Sacred Well of Chichén-Itzá, Mexico
- ☑ Climb Ayers Rock in Australia
- ☑ Follow River Jordan from Sea of Galilee to Dead Sea

ACCOMPLISH:

- ☑ Become an Eagle Scout
- ☑ Dive in a submarine
- ☑ Land on and take off from an aircraft carrier
- ☑ Fly in a blimp, balloon, and glider
- ☑ Ride an elephant, camel, ostrich, and bronco
- ☑ Skin dive to 40 feet and hold breath 2.5 minutes underwater
- ☑ Catch a ten-pound lobster and a ten-inch abalone
- ☑ Play flute and violin
- ☑ Type 50 words a minute
- ☑ Make a parachute jump
- ☑ Learn water- and snow skiing
- ☑ Go on a church mission
- ☑ Follow the John Muir Trail
- ☑ Study native medicines and bring back useful ones
- ☑ Bag camera trophies of elephant, lion, rhino, cheetah, cape buffalo, and whale
- ☑ Learn to fence
- ☑ Learn jujitsu
- ☑ Teach a college course
- ☑ Watch a cremation ceremony in Bali
- ☑ Explore depths of the sea
- ☐ Appear in a Tarzan movie
- ☐ Own a horse, chimpanzee, cheetah, ocelot, and coyote (yet to own a chimp or cheetah)
- ☐ Become a ham radio operator
- ☑ Build own telescope
- ☑ Write a book
- ☑ Publish an article in National Geographic magazine

- ☑ High jump five feet
- ☑ Broad-jump 15 feet
- ☑ Run mile in five minutes
- ☐ Carry out careers in medicine and exploration (studied premed, treats illnesses among primitive tribes)
- ☐ Visit every country in the world (30 to go)
- ☑ Study Navaho and Hopi Indians
- ☑ Learn to fly a plane
- ☑ Ride a horse in the Rose Parade
- ☑ Weigh 175 pounds stripped
- ☑ Perform 200 sit-ups and 20 pull-ups
- ☑ Learn French, Spanish, and Arabic
- ☐ Study dragon lizards on Komodo Island (Boat broke down within 20 miles of island)
- ☑ Visit birthplace of Grandfather Sorenson in Denmark
- ☑ Visit birthplace of Grandfather Goddard in England
- ☑ Ship aboard a freighter as a seaman
- ☐ Read the entire Encyclopedia Britannica
- ☑ Read the Bible from cover to cover
- ☑ Read the works of Shakespeare, Plato, Aristotle, Dickens, Thoreau, Rousseau, Conrad, Twain, Hemingway, Burroughs, Talmage, Tolstoy, Longfellow, Keats, Poe, Bacon, Whittier, and Emerson (not every work)
- ☑ Become familiar with the compositions of Bach, Beethoven, Debussy, Ibert, Mendelssohn, Lalo, Liszt, Rimski-Korsakov, Respighi, Rachmaninoff, Paganini, Stravinsky, Toch, Tchaikovsky, Verdi
- ☑ Become proficient in the use of a plane, motor cycle, tractor, surfboard, rifle, pistol, canoe, microscope, football, basketball, bow and arrow, lariat, and boomerang
- ☑ Compose music
- ☑ Play Clair de Lune on the piano
- ☑ Watch fire-walking ceremony (In Bali and Surinam)
- ☑ Milk a poisonous snake (bitten by diamondback during photo session)
- ☑ Light a match with .22 rifle
- ☑ Visit a movie studio
- ☑ Climb Cheops' pyramid
- ☑ Become a member of the Explorer's Club and the Adventure's Club
- ☑ Learn to play polo
- ☑ Travel through the Grand Canyon on foot and by boat
- ☑ Circumnavigate the globe (four times)
- ☐ Visit the moon
- ☑ Marry and have children (has five children)
- ☑ Live to see the 21st century

By the end of the book, you will have created a life list of your own— we call it **Your Dream List**. The following chapters will break down the most important areas of your life and help you focus on specifically what you want to accomplish.

John Goddard had a really strong vision to be an explorer. His list also shows that he values family, physical fitness, literature, and music, and he has some goals or missions related to these values as well. This guide will walk you through figuring out what you value most and turning your values into many missions for your life, as well as help you uncover **your life vision**.

First, let's find out where you are by looking at where you have been . . .

You Were Here. ↓

Your Life So Far

Sometimes, taking a quick look at where you have been helps you understand where you are, and knowing this will give you the starting place to get where you want to be with your life. Take this opportunity to ask yourself a few important questions about your time so far on Planet Earth. Go ahead and answer the following questions on the slips of paper below (or if you don't have enough room, grab some blank paper).

What are the significant events that have shaped your life?

Where were you born?

Where did you grow up?

What type of environment did you live in?

Did you move a lot?

Did your family have any major crises?

Any divorces, deaths, or bankruptcies?

Did you have any major accidents, illnesses or injuries?

Where did you go to school?

Were you ever held back a grade? Ever skip a grade?

Did you have a teacher who was especially challenging or inspiring?

Did you have a favorite class?

Did you have a significant friendship that shaped your path?

Did you have any best friends, pets, girlfriends/boyfriends?

Did you ever fall in love or have your heart broken?

Did anyone close to you die or become seriously ill or injured?

Did you travel anywhere with family, school, organizations, or by yourself?

What was your spiritual life like?

Did you practice any religion?

Any rites of passage (such as confirmation, bar mitzvah, etc)?

Was there a time when you started to believe something new or different from your family?

Did you have any responsibilities or jobs?

Did you have to help around the house?

How did your parents relate to their jobs?

Did they ever change careers?

Did they ever get fired?

Did they like their jobs?

Did any music, book, art, web site, movie, or person open your mind to a new way of thinking?

Did you belong to any groups (such as sports team, church, temple, Scouts, dance troupe, club)?

Were you a leader in any of these organizations?

What was your money situation growing up?

Did your family struggle or did you always have enough money?

Did you have your own car?

Did you have to earn your own money?

Did anyone help you believe in yourself while growing up?

Did anyone encourage you to take a certain career or life path?

Did anyone tell you to give up on a dream or weaken your confidence in yourself?

What to do next?

Star the events that you think made a big impact on you and shaped your life. Go ahead and put these events on the next page on your Life Map.

My Life Map

Use these pages to get creative. Design your Life Map any way you like. Fill in the most significant events that have shaped your life so far (from the previous page) and any dates of the events if you know them. What makes up the map of who you are?

Born Here:

Part 2

My Missions,
Visions,
Strategies,
and Steps

Chapter 1

What matters to you most?

When someone sets out to build a new house, they don't just show up with a load of lumber and tools and a general idea of what to build. First they spend some time thinking about what they want in a home; then they make **detailed plans and drawings** of what the house will look like. Then they come up with a **strategy** for its construction. By now they have a **vision** for how it will feel to live in their new home. And they have clearly defined **steps** for how it's going to happen. Without these necessary steps, they aren't likely to end up with the house they want. Designing your life is a lot like that.

In this section, you will start actively designing your life. You'll begin by finding your most important values, then you'll create your mission and vision statements, and finally, you will develop the strategies for keeping yourself on track. These steps are the foundation for building your life the way you want it to be. This chapter will set you up for the rest of the book, so it's a great place to start.

Do you know what matters to you most?

If **YES**, is this you?
❑ I know what's most important to me and I'm excited about the direction I'm headed in. I've got it all dialed, and everyone I care about is on board with my plan and supports me fully.

Excellent! Sounds as though you have your plan well put together. This chapter should be smooth sailing. These exercises will help you fine-tune your vision with a statement to keep you moving toward your dreams. They'll also help you be sure that your vision is in line with your values.

Or is this you?
❑ I know what matters most to me, but I don't feel that I have the full support of my family, friends, or someone else important in my life.

Have you clearly expressed your vision to all the people in your life? Sometimes a misunderstanding or a perceived lack of support happens simply because the people who care about you don't really know what you want. They may even be going by old information or just by what they see as your natural talents. This chapter will help you form clear, succinct statements that you can share with anyone to explain exactly what direction you're going. You can even give them the whole chapter if you need to!

If **NO**, is this you?
❑ I don't have a *clue* what matters most or even what I want to do with my life.

It's okay—you don't have to have everything figured out. This chapter should help you get started in the right direction just by giving you a better

sense of what matters to you most in life. The later chapters will get more specific, and by then you may have a stronger idea of the direction you're headed in.

Or is this you?
❑ I feel as if I'm going a whole bunch of directions at the same time, and all of them are interesting! I can't make up my mind which way to go.

Definitely go through this chapter and see if it gives you some clarity. If you're planning to go to college right away but are still torn about what direction to go, maybe you can take some required courses that will apply no matter which direction you ultimately decide on. Or you might consider taking some time off to sort out what you're most interested in before investing too much time or money in school. Check out the option of a gap year in chapter 3.

Or is this you?
❑ I'm not really into planning out my life. I think I'll just go where the wind takes me.

That's actually fine, too. You don't have to plan out every last detail and then stick to it. But sometimes it's fun to dream a little, to envision a target and then try to aim for it. Your vision for life may change as you gather new experiences. And having a vision doesn't even mean you're stuck on how it should unfold. If you are clear about the general direction you want to go, you can be flexible with the details and live a rich, exciting life no matter what comes up. Take a look at this first chapter anyway. Maybe you can skip the rest of the book until later, when you're more interested.

My Life Values

Are your friends more important to you than family? Does fame seem more interesting than education? How does having fun compare with working hard? How about inspiration versus financial security?

Your personal values are the things in life that mean the most to you. Some people value inner peace, love, or family above all else, while others would put money, career, or education at the top of their list. There is no "right" list—they're like fingerprints; everyone's will be different. It's really helpful to discover what your core values are, since they will act as a compass, guiding you to what you really want in life. You can better focus your time and energy toward achieving your goals when you begin to base your decisions and actions on your values.

What to do next? Go through the list of values.

✓ Check any that are important to you.   ★ Star the really important ones.

? Question-mark any that make you go "Huh?" You can look those up later or just ignore them.

✎ If an important value is missing, write it in the margins.

Acceptance		Clarity		Entertainment		Growth
Achievement		Cleanliness		Enthusiasm		Happiness
Acknowledgement		Comfort		Excellence		Hard work
Adaptability		Compassion		Excitement		Harmony
Adventure		Competition		Expertise		Health
Affection		Confidence		Exploration		Helpfulness
Agility		Conformity		Expressiveness		Holiness
Alertness		Consciousness		Extravagance		Honesty
Altruism		Control		Fairness		Hospitality
Ambition		Conviction		Faith		Humility
Amusement		Coolness		Fame		Humor
Art		Cooperation		Family		Imagination
Assertiveness		Creativity		Fashion		Independence
Athleticism		Credibility		Financial security		Ingenuity
Attentiveness		Curiosity		Firmness		Inquisitiveness
Awareness		Decisiveness		Fitness		Insightfulness
Balance		Dependability		Flexibility		Inspiration
Beauty		Depth		Focus		Integrity
Being the best		Determination		Fortitude		Intelligence
Belonging		Dignity		Frankness		Interesting experiences
Bravery		Diversity		Freedom		Intimacy
Calmness		Doing the right thing		Friendship		Introversion
Celebrity		Duty		Frugality		Intuition
Challenge		Education		Fun		Innovation
Change		Effectiveness		Generosity		Investing
Charity		Empowerment		Getting ahead		Joy
Chastity		Endurance		Getting my way		Justice
Children		Energy		Grace		Kindness
Cheerfulness		Enlightenment		Gratitude		Knowledge

Leadership	Patriotism	Resolve	Solitude
Learning	Peace	Resourcefulness	Spirituality
Leisure time	Perceptiveness	Respect	Spontaneity
Liberty	Perfection	Rest	Spunk
Liveliness	Perkiness	Restraint	Stability
Logic	Persistence	Reverence	Strength
Longevity	Philanthropy	Sacredness	Success
Love	Playfulness	Sacrifice	Support
Loyalty	Pleasure	Safety	Teamwork
Making a difference	Poise	Satisfaction	Thankfulness
Marriage	Popularity	Security	Thoughtfulness
Mastery	Power	Self-control	Thrift
Material things	Practicality	Self esteem	Tidiness
Maturity	Precision	Self expression	Timeliness
Mellowness	Preparedness	Selflessness	Travel
Meticulousness	Privacy	Self-reliance	Trustworthiness
Mindfulness	Proactiveness	Self respect	Truthfulness
Modesty	Professionalism	Sensitivity	Understanding
Money	Prosperity	Sensuality	Uniqueness
Motivation	Punctuality	Serenity	Unity
Mysteriousness	Realism	Service	Usefulness
Neatness	Reason	Sexuality	Victory
Obedience	Rebellion	Sharing	Vision
Open-mindedness	Recognition	Shrewdness	Vitality
Optimism	Refinement	Silliness	Warmth
Order	Relaxation	Simplicity	Wealth
Organization	Reliability	Sincerity	Winning
Originality	Religiousness	Skill	Wisdom
Outrageousness	Reputation	Socializing	Wit
Passion	Resilience	Solidarity	Youthfulness

Give the list of values you checked one more glance. Are there any that you would change? Don't check it or star it just because you think you should. Remember, we're looking for YOUR values, not your mother's!

Once you've gone through the list a second time, write out the values you starred.

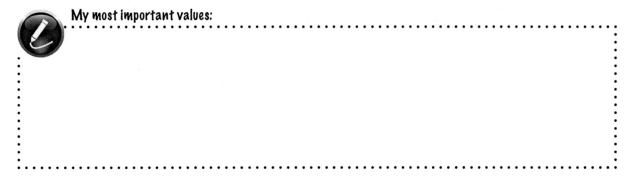

My most important values:

What to do next?

Put your values in order, starting with the most important. Write the top twelve below. Feel free to explain or clarify any of them.

You will be using these in the next few pages to come up with your mission and vision statements.

Jim's List of Values

1. Inspiration
2. Consciousness
3. Passion (for what I do)
4. Optimism
5. Love (of life and for others)
6. Marriage
7. Health
8. Family
9. Friendship
10. Empowerment (of others)
11. Sincerity
12. Humor
13. Generosity
14. Financial security
15. Balance

The values that matter to me most:

#1

#2

#3

#4

#5

#6

#7

#8

#9

#10

#11

#12

Mission Possible

Do you have a mission for your life? Is there something you want to accomplish, or something you care about deeply? Have you ever put it into words, into a mission statement?

All successful businesses have a mission statement. Google's mission, "to organize the world's information and make it universally accessible and useful," gets right to the heart of what they do.

Most people who have achieved greatness have been guided by a personal mission, even if they never wrote it down. Being able to state your own personal mission will help you clarify what your values are and what your real purpose is. Your mission is like a T-shirt that you wear around. It tells everyone what you are about. Most important, it is a reminder of why you are here on Planet Earth.

You can keep your mission inside, but writing it out gives you better clarity and focus. A mission statement should be simple, distilled down to one sentence or, better yet, just a few words. Your mission statement doesn't have to say anything about

how you will accomplish this mission; we'll do that later, in the vision statement.

Your mission may change depending on whom you are with and what you are doing, or just naturally over time as your interests evolve. You'll likely have a different mission for each of the areas of your life that are most important to you. If your top values are family, friends, school, and reputation, each of these values will have a different mission statement. Maybe your mission at school is to be the star athlete, but at home it is to keep your family from driving you crazy. Or perhaps you have a more universal value, like joy or kindness which could apply to most if not all the areas of your life, or just life in general.

On the next page, fill in your top twelve values above each T-shirt and try to write a quick mission statement for each. Then look at the choices below each T-shirt and check any area of your life that your mission seems to apply to. See Jim's example below.

Value: _Inspiration_

To be inspired by life and to inspire others.

☑ Life in general
☑ Career
☑ Education
☑ Home
☑ Relationships
☑ Hobbies/pastimes
☑ Personal development

Value: _Optimism_

To keep a positive outlook on life.

☑ Life in general
☐ Career
☐ Education
☐ Home
☐ Relationships
☐ Hobbies/pastimes
☐ Personal development

Value: _Marriage_

To have a happy, committed, loving marriage.

☐ Life in general
☐ Career
☐ Education
☐ Home
☑ Relationships
☐ Hobbies/pastimes
☐ Personal development

My Life Missions

Whoa, why so many missions? We just wanted to leave you plenty of room for your values in case you couldn't narrow them down. Don't worry we'll be down to one mission in a few minutes. Use as many of the T-shirts as you want, and leave the rest blank if you can't come up with enough missions to fill them.

Value #1: _____

What areas in your life does this mission affect?
- ❏ Life in general
- ❏ Career
- ❏ Education
- ❏ Home
- ❏ Relationships
- ❏ Hobbies/pastimes
- ❏ Personal development

Value #2: _____

What areas in your life does this mission affect?
- ❏ Life in general
- ❏ Career
- ❏ Education
- ❏ Home
- ❏ Relationships
- ❏ Hobbies/pastimes
- ❏ Personal development

Value #3: _____

What areas in your life does this mission affect?
- ❏ Life in general
- ❏ Career
- ❏ Education
- ❏ Home
- ❏ Relationships
- ❏ Hobbies/pastimes
- ❏ Personal development

Value #4: _____

What areas in your life does this mission affect?
- ❏ Life in general
- ❏ Career
- ❏ Education
- ❏ Home
- ❏ Relationships
- ❏ Hobbies/pastimes
- ❏ Personal development

Value #5: _____

What areas in your life does this mission affect?
- ❏ Life in general
- ❏ Career
- ❏ Education
- ❏ Home
- ❏ Relationships
- ❏ Hobbies/pastimes
- ❏ Personal development

Value #6: _____

What areas in your life does this mission affect?
- ❏ Life in general
- ❏ Career
- ❏ Education
- ❏ Home
- ❏ Relationships
- ❏ Hobbies/pastimes
- ❏ Personal development

Value #7: _____

What areas in your life
does this mission affect?
- ❑ Life in general
- ❑ Career
- ❑ Education
- ❑ Home
- ❑ Relationships
- ❑ Hobbies/pastimes
- ❑ Personal development

Value #8: _____

What areas in your life
does this mission affect?
- ❑ Life in general
- ❑ Career
- ❑ Education
- ❑ Home
- ❑ Relationships
- ❑ Hobbies/pastimes
- ❑ Personal development

Value #9: _____

What areas in your life
does this mission affect?
- ❑ Life in general
- ❑ Career
- ❑ Education
- ❑ Home
- ❑ Relationships
- ❑ Hobbies/pastimes
- ❑ Personal development

Value #10: _____

What areas in your life
does this mission affect?
- ❑ Life in general
- ❑ Career
- ❑ Education
- ❑ Home
- ❑ Relationships
- ❑ Hobbies/pastimes
- ❑ Personal development

Value #11: _____

What areas in your life
does this mission affect?
- ❑ Life in general
- ❑ Career
- ❑ Education
- ❑ Home
- ❑ Relationships
- ❑ Hobbies/pastimes
- ❑ Personal development

Value #12: _____

What areas in your life
does this mission affect?
- ❑ Life in general
- ❑ Career
- ❑ Education
- ❑ Home
- ❑ Relationships
- ❑ Hobbies/pastimes
- ❑ Personal development

Now it's time to come up with your primary mission. This is the one main mission that keeps you really jazzed about life.

Here are a few different ways you can write your primary mission:
1. Pick the most important mission from the previous page.
2. Combine a few of your individual missions into one cohesive mission.
3. Come up with something completely different from your other missions that better describes your primary purpose.

As an example, there's Jim's primary mission to the right. How did he come up with it? After seeing how many areas of his life his value of inspiration affected, Jim decided to use that as his primary mission and build on it. He took a look at his other values and saw that empowering others and having a positive outlook on life were in the top ten as well. Ultimately he chose something based on his passion— a feeling that resonated in his heart, which is what we want to encourage you to do too.

My Primary Life Mission:

A Vision for Life

If your mission statement is the T-shirt you wear around proclaiming your purpose, the vision is like a pair of glasses you wear to see your mission. The vision is the focus, the clarity of your purpose. Your vision statement spells out the unique and specific ways that you see yourself accomplishing your purpose. Like your mission, your vision will evolve over time as you develop new skills and interests.

Two people can have exactly the same mission statement, but usually the vision statement shows where their focus differs. Many different visions can fulfill the same mission. Let's say one of your missions is to have a lot of money. There are an infinite number of visions that could go with that mission: write a bestselling novel, design a new type of kayak, invest in an Internet company, become a neurosurgeon, or even inherit the money. There are no right answers here, and no wrong ones. You are designing your vision based on what feels right to *you*.

Your vision statement doesn't have to get too wordy. Keep it simple and focused. If you aren't sure of the specifics right now, you can make a general statement. Say you know you want to help people in some capacity but don't know exactly how you would go about it. Go ahead and state your vision as best you can. Writing it down gives it more power than it could ever have as just a thought or image floating around in your head. You may even find that by writing it out, you realize that you don't want to follow the path had been thinking of—and that's a good thing to know, right? This guide is meant to be part of your learning process.

Here are a few examples of general vision statements based on Jim's values list:

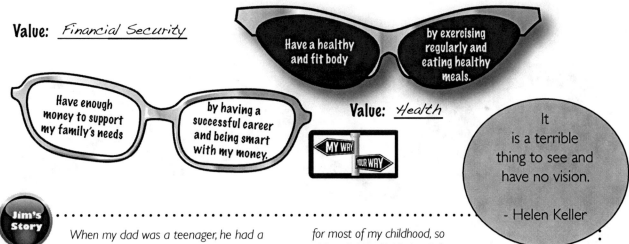

Value: Financial Security

Have enough money to support my family's needs by having a successful career and being smart with my money.

Have a healthy and fit body by exercising regularly and eating healthy meals.

Value: Health

It is a terrible thing to see and have no vision.

- Helen Keller

Jim's Story

When my dad was a teenager, he had a vision of becoming a famous rock star. He was in a popular band during high school and had a few potential leads for a career as a musician. His most important value has always been his family, and his primary mission was someday to be a loving, supportive husband and father and a good provider. He couldn't see a way to balance his primary mission with his vision of being a rock star, so after graduation the band broke up and he pursued a way to make a living. He didn't have a specific vision for how he would provide for his family, so he followed the same path as many of his friends: he took a good-paying job in the factories. He accomplished his mission, but he worked the three-to-midnight shift for most of my childhood, so although he provided well for the family financially, he couldn't be with us as much as he would have liked. Recently when we were talking, he told me that if he had taken the time to clarify his vision when he was younger, he might have found a way to bring together his mission and vision in the form of a more satisfying career. Now that Dad is nearing retirement, he's beginning to wonder what he might do with this next stage of his life. While we might not see him touring the top venues around the country anytime soon, I wouldn't be surprised if he got the old Fender Stratocaster out of the closet before too long!

My Visions

Take each of your twelve missions and form it into a brief vision statement. Remember that a vision statement tells how you will accomplish your mission. You may find it easier for you to get started if you write each mission statement in the lens on the left and then fill in the rest on the right side.

Vision statements don't have to be boring—although we have read plenty of boring business visions in our day. They need to keep you looking forward to your future, so they should be exciting for you, and challenging for you, but also attainable. The later chapters are divided up in a way that allows you to create visions specific to to education, making a living, taking time off, finding a place to fit in, relationships, travel, spirituality, and hobbies. This part will get more specific and more personalized as you start to lay out the ideas that will form your Dream List at the end of the book.

The visions on this page are based on your life values, so they may sound less specific and more universal than the later ones. You may have a bunch of friends with a similar value for friendship (hopefully, right?), and your vision could be something like this:

To have friends who are fun to be around, who make me laugh, whom I can totally trust, and whom I can repay by being a loyal friend myself.

Don't worry you'll have a chance to express yourself and your uniqueness very soon. In fact, it's probably coming through already in your statements, especially your primary mission statement.

If you think you need more information to fill in these visions, you can come back to this section after you've sorted out your specific visions in the later chapters.

#1:

#2:

#3:

#4:

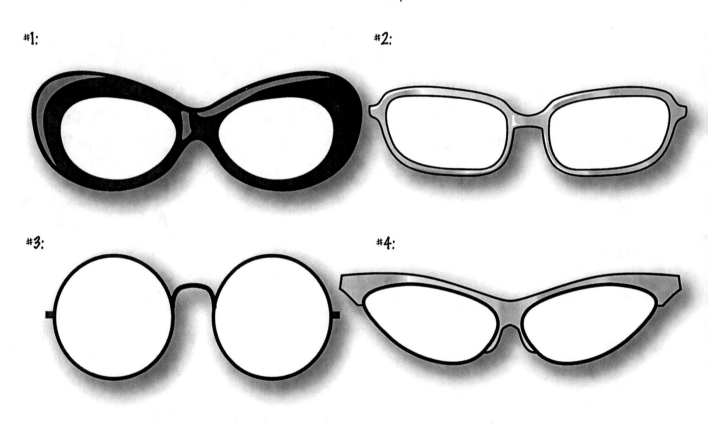

#5:

#6:

#7:

#8:

#9:

#10:

#11:

#12:

Here are some examples of mission and vision statements with a bit more "zazz".

Just as you created a primary mission from your individual missions, now it's time to formulate your life vision. So...what's a life vision?

Your life vision represents how you want to accomplish your main purpose in life, and it's usually based on your primary mission. It may incorporate any of your individual visions, but its most important function is to represent the big vision—the one that keeps you focused on, and stoked about, your future.

In Jim's vision, he incorporates many of his missions together, including his career, his marriage, and his loftier values of inspiration, passion, and optimism. Here's Jim's life vision:

There are quite a few different ways you can write your life vision:
1. Use your primary mission statement to create your life vision.
2. Pick the vision from the previous page that stands out the most.
3. Combine a few of your individual visions into one cohesive, overarching vision.

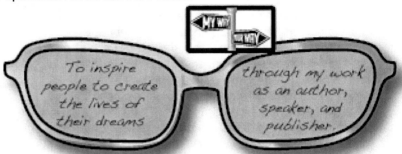

My Life Vision:

We think it's possible to line up your values with your mission AND your vision so that every part of your life feels satisfying and fulfilling.

But it takes a little focus...

And maybe some strategies...

When Jim was growing up, his grandpa told him: *"Life is not about doing what you like; life is about learning to like what you have to do."*

This piece of advice is a life strategy. It guided the way that Jim's grandpa lived. When life was tough, he used this strategy as a way to persevere and put food on the table.

Growing up, you learned life strategies from your family members, teachers, friends, and society. Very often your values come from the life strategies that were repeated frequently. If someone told you, "Money doesn't grow on trees," you may have adopted the value of frugality. If you always heard, "If at first you don't succeed, try again," you may see perseverance as one of your main values. The motto "Family always comes first" may have made family your number one value.

If you get a piece of advice that is consistent with your life experience (it makes sense to you), you will probably adopt the value and strategy as your own. But if the advice *doesn't* agree with what you believe to be true, you'll probably form a new strategy for life. While Jim appreciated his grandpa's advice, his exposure to new people and new ways of living helped change his strategy to:

"Life is about discovering what you love to do and finding a way to do it!"

It's natural for each new generation to modify the advice of the generation that came before it. Ask your parents how their life strategies differ from what their parents advised. Generally, your core values coincide with your parents', but the strategies you choose for living your life will probably differ.

Strategies are like road signs that keep you aligned with your values and on course with your mission and your vision. Depending on your mission and the people around you, you may use multiple strategies to accomplish your goals. You generally use strategies when you hit a challenge, something that gets in the way of your goals. When the pressure is on, sometimes you default to old strategies, which maybe never helped you in the first place. That's why right now is a good time to come up with strategies to get you through life's challenges—while you aren't in the middle of those challenges.

Here are some examples of strategies and the values that are tied to them:

My Life Strategies

Which strategies have you used in the past? Think about the ways you usually respond to a challenging situation. Sometimes a voice pops into your head (it may sound a lot like your parents), giving you a word of guidance about what to do next. If you need more help, look at the examples on the previous page. Fill in a few strategies that have guided your life so far:

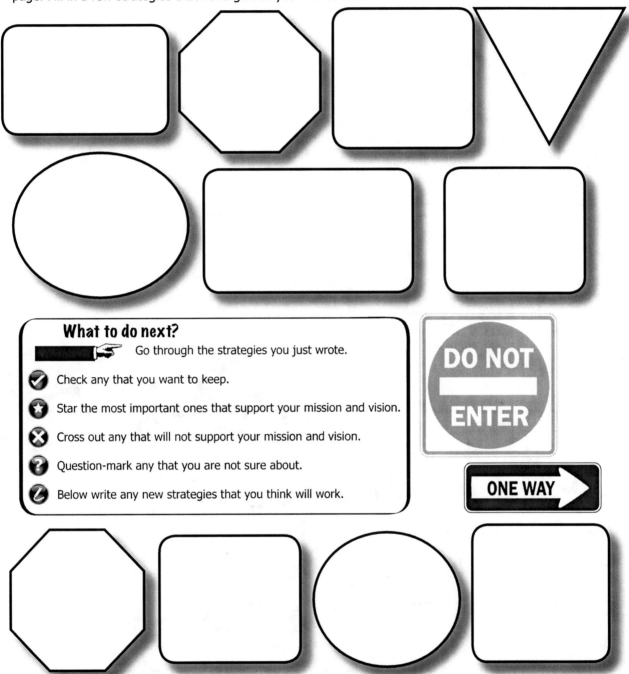

What to do next?

☞ Go through the strategies you just wrote.

✔ Check any that you want to keep.

★ Star the most important ones that support your mission and vision.

✘ Cross out any that will not support your mission and vision.

❓ Question-mark any that you are not sure about.

✎ Below write any new strategies that you think will work.

DO NOT ENTER

ONE WAY ➤

Your values, mission, vision, and strategies are the solid foundation on which you will build the rest of your life. From now on, whenever you have a question about whether you want to do a particular thing with your time, energy, or money, you can check in with these fundamentals and make a decision, confident that it is aligned with who you are and what you stand for.

Before you move on to the next chapter, there is one last detail to look at: steps toward your vision...

Steps toward My Vision

If you have created a solid life vision, it's time to start making plans on how you are going to turn your ideas into your everyday reality. If you haven't established your life vision, come back to this section later.

Most people spend hours planning vacations, parties, and weddings but tend to spend a lot less time making detailed plans for much bigger areas of their lives, like education, career, and family.

Plans include the steps you intend to take toward accomplishing your vision. We're not suggesting that you map out every teensy detail of your life right here, because, as they say, "the joy is in the journey." But once you've discovered your vision, planning at least the first few steps helps get you moving in the right direction. It can take years, maybe even a lifetime, to fulfill your vision, but having a list of steps that you can check off one by one will give you a sense of satisfaction and reinforce your desire to keep moving forward with your plan.

Jim's example lists only his major steps, leaving out many of the smaller, day-to-day details of writing a book, researching how to run a publishing company, and learning how to market his ideas. You can make your plan as detailed as you like, whether laying out every single step or focusing only on the major goals you will achieve along the way.

Steps to Jim's Life Vision

1. *Launching the new Web site.*

2. *Presenting the first college workshop.*

3. *Delivering the first graduation speech.*

4. *Giving away the first Gap Year Scholarship.*

5. *Selling the first 5,000 copies.*

6. *Making the first appearance on Oprah.*

Ease the pain and suffering of people in need **by becoming a doctor and starting a free health clinic overseas.**

Step #1
Apply to undergraduate colleges and get accepted by one with a good pre-med program.

Step #2
Apply and get accepted by a medical school.

Step #3
Choose a specialty that would be useful in an area with very few resources.

Step #4
Graduate with an M.D.

Step #5
Land a residency in a reputable hospital.

Step #6
Work for a few years in a local hospital to pay off student loans.

Step #7
Research and apply to an overseas program such as the Peace Corps or Doctors without Borders.

Step #8
Establish a medical clinic in a developing country.

Sometimes steps don't need to be taken in a particular order. If this is true for you, feel free to jump around according to what inspires you in the moment. Steps can be abandoned when they no longer support your vision or when the flow of life leads you down a different path. As John Lennon said, "Life is what happens to you when you're busy making other plans." When you are aligned with your vision, new paths that you never could have imagined will open up for you. So stay alert, be flexible with your steps, and keep focused on your vision.

Use the space below to write out the most important steps that will lead you to your life vision. This will get you started, but you may have hundreds of smaller steps in between. If you need to, you can always use more paper or your computer to lay it out in more detail.

Step #1

Step #2

Step #3

Step #4

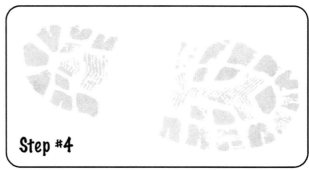

Step #5

Step #6

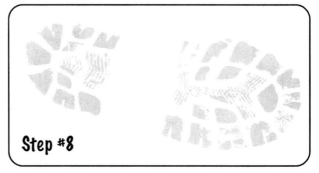

Step #7

Step #8

You will be using the information in this chapter throughout the rest of the book as you explore what you would like to learn, how you'd like to make a living, where you want to live, and what keeps you going. Refer to these pages whenever you need to remind yourself what matters to you most (as we sometimes forget), but don't feel bound by what you've written here. These things often change as you learn more about yourself and have new experiences.

You can't teach
a man anything;
you can only help him
discover it in himself.

—Galileo

Chapter 2

What do you want to know?

Learning is a lifelong process regardless of whether you want to pursue any further education. Let's check in about what you want to learn in this lifetime and how you want to learn it.

Are you planning to go to college right away?

If **YES**, is this you?
❑ I'm excited and can't wait to start college.

Or is this you?
❑ My parents are "making" me go.

Is there some other reason for starting school now?
❑ If I don't go to college immediately after high school, I'll lose momentum and maybe never get back to it.
❑ I can't find a good job without a college education.
❑ I want to go to college just to get away from my family.

Whatever your answer, start with the values on the next page and get clear on what your reasons are for going back to school.

If **NO**, is this you?
❑ I have other plans (military, travel, volunteer service)
❑ I need a break from school for a little while.

There's a lot you can learn through real-life experience, traveling the world, and meeting new people. Check out the option of a gap year in chapter 3.

Or is this you?
❑ I'm not smart enough to go to college.
❑ I don't want to leave someone behind.
❑ I don't have the money to pay for college.
❑ Nobody in my family has ever gone to college.

It sounds as though there may be a roadblock in the way of your vision. Check out roadblocks and detours in chapter 8.

Or is this you?
❑ I already finished a college degree.

Congratulations! If you think you may want to do advanced studies, read on. If you're satisfied with your degree and ready to prepare for your career, skip to chapter 4. If you need to take some time off, visit chapter 3 first.

Regardless of whether you want to go to college right away or not, **do you know *what* you want to know?**

If **YES**, is this you?
❑ There's a specific field of study that I am eager to learn in college.

Start with values and work your way through this chapter. You may skip the subjects list, or you might stop there briefly to see if there are any other things you want to learn.

Or is this you?
❑ I have a career in mind and I don't need to go to college.

Glance through this chapter, but you may want to skip it and go on to chapter 4, "How do you want to make a living?".

Or is this you?
❑ I have a job lined up after high school and don't really care about having a career in something I'm interested in. I just need to pay the bills.

Skip this chapter entirely, and try out one of the later ones, maybe chapter 5, "Where in the world do you fit in?" or chapter 6, "Who do you want to spend your life with?"

If **NO**, is this you?
❑ I don't have a clue what major to study in college.
❑ I don't know what type of career I want yet.
❑ I'm interested in a lot of subjects, but I don't know which to pursue.

In all these cases, check out the subjects list in the following pages to look at your interests. Then you may want to start with chapter 4, "How do you want to make a living?" and uncover your skills before coming back to this chapter.

> **If none of these answers seem to fit, skim through this chapter to see if it interests you. You can always come back to it later.**

Values and Choices for My Education

Maybe prestige figures highly in your values, and you want to attend an Ivy League college. Or it may be more important for you to stay out of debt and find a school with low tuition and an opportunity for work-study. Perhaps attending a school where most of your friends will be is more important than going somewhere far from home. Or your values for education may be tied to getting a good-paying job right out of school, so you can support your family.

You determined your life values in the previous chapter, and they can be applied to many categories, such as your education and career preferences. You may want to look back on your top eight values now.

The list below incorporates some of the ideas from the life values list, but it gets a lot more specific about your choices and values for education. Even if you're pretty sure where you are going to college, this activity may help you double-check that your decision is in line with your values.

What to do next? Go through the list of values.

✓ Check any that are important to you. ★ Star the really important ones.

? Question-mark any that make you go "Huh?" You can look those up later or just ignore them.

✎ If an important value is missing, write it in the margins.

Cost and Services	Trade school	Marine Corps affiliation
Childcare available	Well-rounded curriculum	Navy affiliation
High tuition	**Facilities and Amenities**	Private school
Low tuition	Clean facilities	Public school
Public transportation available	Comfortable dorm rooms	Religious institution
Scholarship opportunities	Environmentally friendly buildings	ROTC
Student loans	Excellent library	Secular institution
Work my way through school	Good dorm food	Single gender
Work-study available	Great bookstore	Two-year college
Educational Emphasis	Health care center	Well-known school
Arts emphasis	Newer buildings	**Learning Style and Standards**
Career placement	Off-campus housing	Alternative class structure and grading
Environmental awareness	Older buildings	Apprentice-style learning
Foreign language opportunities	Recreation center	Big classes (100+ students)
High-tech emphasis	Beautifully landscaped quad	Challenging
Internship opportunities	**Institution Preferences**	Competitive
Master's degree programs	African-American school	Easy
Medical school	Air Force affiliation	Experienced teachers
Music, dance, performance emphasis	Army affiliation	High admissions standards
On-the-job training	Been around for a long time	Honors program
PhD programs	Coed	Lecture classes
Research emphasis	Four-year college	Live classes
Science emphasis	Good reputation	Lower admissions standards
Seminary	Ivy League	Online classes

Small class discussions	**Student Life and Culture**	Intramural sports
Small classes	Allowed to have a car	Leadership opportunities
Traditional grading and class structure	Bar scene	New friends
Wide choice of majors	Big sports program	Nightlife
Location	City life	Open-minded
Beautiful surroundings	Clubs and organizations	Party school
Far from home	Conformity important	Political activism
In-state	Creativity encouraged	Relaxed
International	Discipline important	Religious groups
Near family	Drug-free campus (relatively)	Safe
Near friends	Ethnic diversity	School newspaper
Near home	Exclusive	Self-expression encouraged
Rural location	Family-friendly	Serious school (less party emphasis)
Urban Location	Fraternities	Small sports program
Within USA	Fun	Sororities
Size	Gay-and-lesbian friendly	Student government
Big population (10,000+ students)	Greek life not emphasized	Study-abroad programs
Really big population (50,000+	Hospitable	Tolerant
Small population	Inclusive	Volunteer programs

When you go through the list, search for that "Right on" or "Are you serious?" response that comes from your initial feeling about a subject. This is explained more on page 136. When you are finished, write out the starred list of values below.

The most important values and choices for my education:

Now put your values and choices in order, starting with the most important.

#1

#2

#3

#4

#5

#6

#7

#8

Use your most important values to come up with five mission statements specific to education. There are some examples on the next page.

If you checked
☑ Education
under any missions on pages 24-25, you can fill those in here as well.

My primary mission:

From your smaller mission statements, write one primary mission for your education. Remember that you can use the most important mission statement to represent your primary mission, or you can combine several.

If your mission or vision doesn't feel very strong or clear, you may be forcing the idea of going to school right now. Or you may just need a little more time to sort out what your focus is for your education. There is no sense wasting your time and energy on something that you aren't fully on board with.

Here are a few mission and vision statements:

Have a good time and meet a lot of great people.

Get as far away from home as possible!

Get as far away from home as possible

by attending college in Scotland and traveling throughout Europe.

Have a good time and meet a lot of great people

who will be my lifelong friends.

Figure out what I'm interested in.

Figure out what I'm interested in

and choose my major by the end of my first year of college.

Graduate with a tangible skill that I can take to the job market.

Graduate with a tangible skill as an electrician

apprentice for three months, and enter the workforce.

Be the first person in my family to get a master's degree.

Be the first person in my family to get a master's degree—

in education, at Dartmouth College.

Be trained as a nurse.

Be trained as a nurse at the University of Washington

and have a job lined up immediately after graduation.

Now that you've written your primary mission statement, create your primary vision statement. Remember, the vision statement shows the unique way that you see yourself accomplishing your mission. The vision could expand on where you want to go to school, what you want to study, what part of the country or world you want to be in, or a goal for after graduation. It should get more specific and leave you feeling more focused.

Beth's Story

Since I was my high school class valedictorian, I thought I was expected to start college immediately after graduation. I was never completely sure about my decision to start school right away. I had a group of friends who were taking a year off after high school to travel abroad, and their opportunities seemed infinitely more exciting than mine. Most important, I had no vision for my college education and no idea what I would do after I finished. In fact, I chose my college major during my junior year of high school, based on a ten-minute conversation with a boyfriend at the end of a date. He said he was going to major in psychology, and after he told me a little bit about the subject, I decided I would, too.

Looking back, there's nothing I would change. I wouldn't be where I am now if I had done anything different, and I love my life! But there were many times when I felt I was living life "by default" instead of living with a vision for my future.

If I had any missions at the time for going to school, the top three would be to continue learning, to express myself and discover the freedom of living on my own, and to do what I thought was expected of me. Going to college seemed the easiest option for fulfilling these missions, especially the last one. I graduated after four years with a bachelor's degree in psychology and soon discovered that it left me with no real possibilities for a job right out of college. At that point, I wasn't any closer to deciding what I wanted to do with my life than I had been in high school. So I took a year off to volunteer with Habitat for Humanity and give myself some time to think about what my next step would be.

Going to college without a clue isn't all bad, mind you. There's a lot you can discover about yourself when you're out of your parents' house and on your own. I began to form my own opinions about things I saw around me: politics, religion, race, and women's issues. I was exposed to new and diverse people. I volunteered for and led many organizations, which gave me some great real-world experience. I had an opportunity to take all kinds of classes, and I learned a lot. Above all, I began to learn that it was up to me to make my own decisions, that what I did with my time was my choice. College ended up being a stepping-stone to help me figure out what my life's vision was, but it took quite a few years of being unfocused, and a few more years to pay back all my student loans, to learn these lessons.

Maybe you can save yourself some time, money, and frustration by looking at your values, mission, vision, and strategies for your education now.

Strategies for My Education

Just as you use strategies to guide you through life and keep you on track with your life's vision, certain strategies will help get you through your education. If your vision is to graduate magna cum laude ("with great distinction"), then achieving perfect grades and maintaining a high GPA may be more important to you than having a well-rounded education. You may operate by the strategy "GPA is everything." On the other hand, if friendship is a key value in your life, you may operate by the strategy

that "the best friends you'll ever make will be those from college," and your vision may focus on having a great time with friends rather than on your studies.

Below are some examples of educational strategies. A strategy is often an opinion of what works for one person, and some of the statements below are quotes. Once a strategy works for you, you may want to adopt it as your own and use it to guide your life.

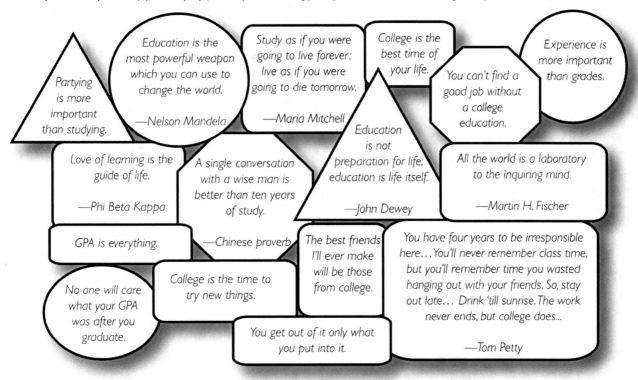

Partying is more important than studying.

Education is the most powerful weapon which you can use to change the world.
—Nelson Mandela

Study as if you were going to live forever; live as if you were going to die tomorrow.
—Maria Mitchell

College is the best time of your life.

You can't find a good job without a college education.

Experience is more important than grades.

Love of learning is the guide of life.
—Phi Beta Kappa

A single conversation with a wise man is better than ten years of study.
—Chinese proverb

Education is not preparation for life; education is life itself.
—John Dewey

All the world is a laboratory to the inquiring mind.
—Martin H. Fischer

GPA is everything.

The best friends I'll ever make will be those from college.

You have four years to be irresponsible here…You'll never remember class time, but you'll remember time you wasted hanging out with your friends. So, stay out late… Drink 'till sunrise. The work never ends, but college does…
—Tom Petty

No one will care what your GPA was after you graduate.

College is the time to try new things.

You get out of it only what you put into it.

What are your strategies for learning? Do you use any of the above, or do your learning strategies fit with your life strategies on page 35? Go ahead and fill in some of the education strategies that are aligned with your values, your mission, and your vision for learning.

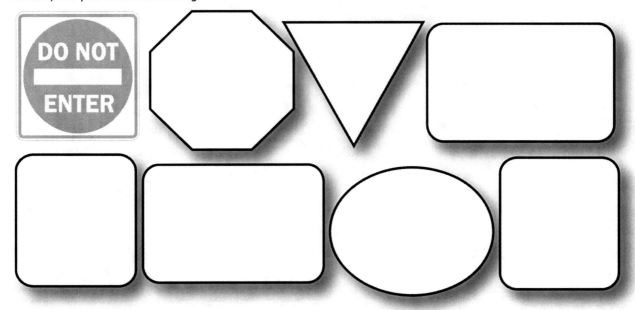

What do you want to know?   45

Steps for My Education

Now is the time to map out the steps that you think will be most important for you to pursue your vision for learning. Remember to base your steps on the primary vision statement you created on the last page.

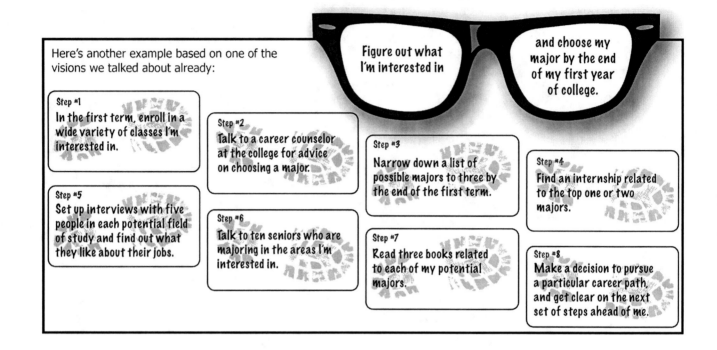

Here's another example based on one of the visions we talked about already:

Figure out what I'm interested in and choose my major by the end of my first year of college.

Step #1
In the first term, enroll in a wide variety of classes I'm interested in.

Step #2
Talk to a career counselor at the college for advice on choosing a major.

Step #3
Narrow down a list of possible majors to three by the end of the first term.

Step #4
Find an internship related to the top one or two majors.

Step #5
Set up interviews with five people in each potential field of study and find out what they like about their jobs.

Step #6
Talk to ten seniors who are majoring in the areas I'm interested in.

Step #7
Read three books related to each of my potential majors.

Step #8
Make a decision to pursue a particular career path, and get clear on the next set of steps ahead of me.

The journey of a thousand miles begins with one step.

—Lao Tzu

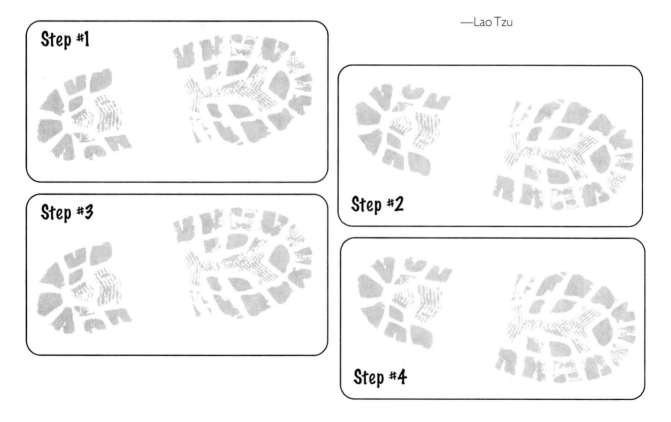

Step #1

Step #2

Step #3

Step #4

Step #5

Step #6

Step #7

Step #8

Step #9

Step #10

Step #11

Step #12

Step #13

Step #14

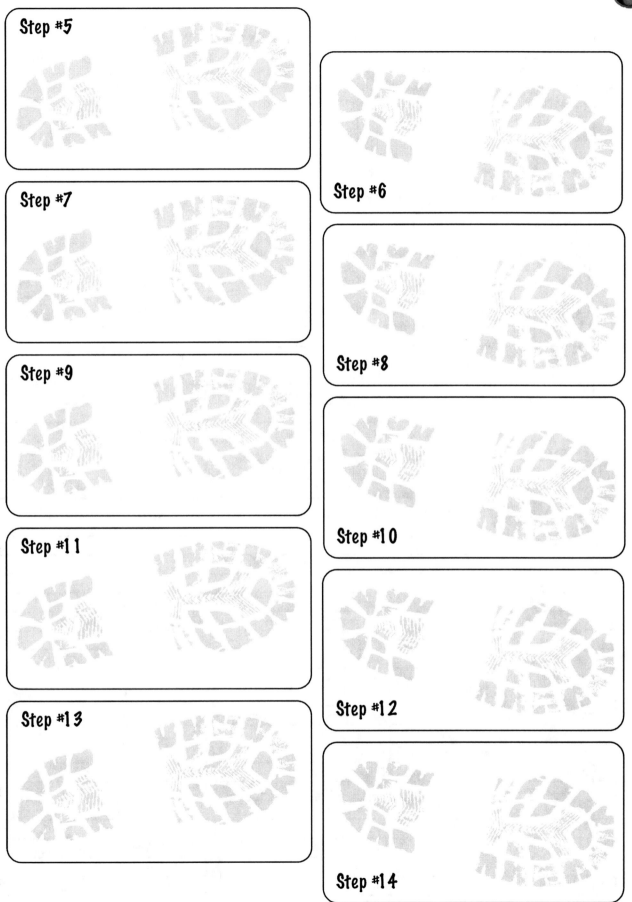

So Many Subjects, So Little Time

There are enough subjects in this world to keep you studying for the rest of your life. You can learn as broadly or as specifically as you like. You can study as a hobby or get your PhD and become a leading researcher in a particular field. Are you being called to further education? If so, run through the list of subjects below. This list has been pulled from a number of four-year colleges and universities as well as trade schools, but it still represents a very small sampling of the areas you can study. And it doesn't include the infinitude of subjects you can study on your own. There is a more comprehensive list from the National Center of Education Statistics on the links page at www.wheresthemap.com, if this doesn't cut it.

What to do next? 👉 Go through the list of subjects

✔ Check the subjects you're interested in.

★ Star the subjects you would really like to study, perhaps for a lifetime.

✘ Cross out any subjects you aren't interested in or simply ignore them.

? Question-mark the subjects you don't know anything about but would like to look up later.

✎ Write in the margins any subjects you don't see listed here, and star or check them.

3D Design	Applied Mathematics	Business Administration
Accounting	Applied Music	Business Information Systems
Acting	Architectural Engineering	Business Law
Actuarial Science	Architecture & Urban Planning	Byzantine Studies
Acupuncture & Oriental Medicine	Aromatherapy	Cable Networking
Addictions Work	Art & Design	Calculus
Administrative Support	Art History & Studio Art	Call Center Management
Advanced Electronics	Asian Studies	Calligraphy
Advanced Enterprise Applications	Astronomy	Canadian Studies
Advertising & Design	Athletic Coaching	Cancer Cell Biology
Aesthetics, Skin Care, Electrolysis	Athletic Training	Cardiology
African American Studies	Audio Engineering	Cardio-Phlebotomy
African Studies	Audiology	Cartooning
Agricultural Business	Auditing	Catering Management
Agricultural Science	Automotive Technology	Cell Biology
Agriculture Industry	Aviation	Ceramics
Air Conditioning, Refrigeration	Aviation Maintenance	Chemical Physics
Airbrush	Baking & Pastry	Chemistry
Airframe & Powerplant	Bilingual Education	Chiropractic
Airline Travel Specialist	Biochemistry/Molecular Biology	Choreography
Alternative Medicine	Bioengineering	Cinematography
American Government	Biological Sciences	Civil Engineering
Anesthesiology	Biophysics	Classical Civilizations
Animal Science	Biostatistics	Clinical Laboratory Science
Animation	Blacksmithing	Coastal Navigation
Anthropology	Book Arts	Cognitive Science
Antiquing	Book Keeping	Colonic Hydrotherapy
Antitrust Law	Botany	Commercial Art
Apparel, Merchandising & Design	Broadcasting	Commercial Delivery Driving

Commercial Law	Dental Hygienist Certification	Exhibit Design
Communication Studies	Dentistry/Oral Medicine	Eyelash Extension
Community Development	Dermatology	Family & Children's Law
Community Health Education	Desktop & Web Publishing	Family & Consumer Sciences
Comparative Literature	Developmental Biology	Family Medicine
Comparative Medicine	Dialysis	Fashion Design & Marketing
Comparative Religion	Dietetics	Federal Law & Federalism
Computer Aided Design	Digital Art & Design	Feminist Studies
Computer & Network Servicing	Digital Imaging	Feng Shui
Computer & Telecommunications	Drafting	Fibers/Textiles/Weaving
Computer Design	Drawing	Film & Television Studies
Computer Engineering	Earth & Planetary Sciences	Film & Video
Computer Management	East Asian Civilizations	Finance
Computer Networking	Ecology	Financial Institutions
Computer Office Technologies	E-Commerce	Financial Planning
Computer Programming	Economic Development	Fine Arts
Computer Repair	Economics	Fisheries Biology
Computer Science	Education (Early Childhood)	Floral Design
Computer System Security	Education (Elementary)	Folkart
Computer Technical Support	Education (Secondary)	Folklore & Mythology
Conflict Resolution	Education (Special)	Food Industry Management
Consciousness Studies	Electrical Engineering	Food, Nutrition & Dietetics
Conservation	Electrocardiography	Forensic Chemistry
Constitutional Theory	Emergency Management	French
Construction Management	Emergency Medicine	Furniture Design
Contemplative Education	Employment & Labor Law	Game Software Development
Control Systems Technology	Enameling	Gastroenterology
Corporate Law	Engineering Management	Gender Studies
Cosmetology	Engineering Technology	Genetics
Counseling	English & American Literature	Genome Sciences
Court Reporting	Enterprise Applications Developer	Geography
Creative Writing	Entertainment Business	General Internal Medicine
Criminal Justice	Entrepreneurship	Geology
Criminal Law & Procedure	Environmental Chemistry	German
Critical Reasoning	Environmental Design	Gerontology
Cross-Cultural Literacy	Environmental Education	Glass
Culinary Arts	Environmental Health	Global Health
Culinary Management	Environmental History	Government
Cultural Anthropology	Environmental Law	Graphic Art & Design
Customer Support	Environmental Planning	Graphic Communication
Cyberlaw & Technology	Environment & Public Policy	Hair Design, Barbering
Dance	Environment & Engineering	Hand & Foot Therapy
Database Development	Ethics	Health & Social Behavior
Database Management	Ethnic Studies	Health Education
Decorative Arts	European Studies	Health Information Management
Dental Assisting	Exercise Science	Health Law

Health Policy & Management	Journalism	Medical Business
Healthcare Administration	Jurisprudence	Medical Education
Healthcare Reimbursement	Justice Business Technician	Medical History and Ethics
Healtheology/Metaphysics	Kinesiology	Medical Illustration
Helicopter Flight	Landscape Architecture	Medical Radiography
Herbal Studies	Language & Literacy	Medical Sonography
History	Latin	Medical Specialization
Holistic Health, Homeopathy	Latin American Studies	Medical Transcription
Holistic Skin Care	Law & Economics	Medieval Studies
Holography	Law & Justice	Meditative Arts
Homeland Security	Law Enforcement Administration	Mental Health Counseling
Horticulture	Learning & Teaching	Merchandising
Hotel & Restaurant Management	Legal Assisting	Metalworking
Human Development - Family	Legal Ethics	Meteorology
Human Resources Management	Legal History	Microbiology
HVAC	Legal Nurse Consultant	Microsoft Certification
Hypnotherapy, Parapsychics	Legal Office Administration	Middle Eastern Studies
Illustration	Legal Office Technology	Midwifery
Immunology	Legal Studies	Military Science
Indigenous Peoples Studies	Lesbian & Gay Studies	Mind, Brain, & Behavior
Industrial Instrumentation	Lettering	Mind, Brain, & Education
Industrial Technology	Life Coaching	Molecular & Cellular Biology
Infectious Disease	Lighting	Molecular Genetics
Information Security	Linguistics	Multiculturalism
Information Systems	Literary Criticism	Museum Studies
Information Technology	Literature & Language	Music
Inner Asian & Altaic Studies	Local Government Law	Music Business
Instructional Design	Makeup	Music Therapy
Instructional Media	Management Info Systems	Musical Theater
Instructor Training	Manufacturing Engineering	Mythology
Insurance	Marbling	Native American Studies
Insurance Billing	Marine Biology	Natural History
Intellectual Property	Marine Mechanics	Natural Resource Management
Interactive Media	Marine Science	Near East Language & Civilization
Interior & Environmental Design	Marketing	Negotiation & Mediation
International Development	Marriage & Family Therapy	Nephrology
International Education Policy	Mass Communication	Neurobiology
International Management	Massage Therapy	Neurology
International Relations	Mathematical Biology	Nuclear Medical Technology
International Studies	Mathematics	Nursing
Iridology	Mechanical & Materials Sciences	Nutrition
IT Management	Media Arts	Obstetrics and Gynecology
Italian	Media Production	Occupational Therapy
Japanese	Medical Administration	Office Administration/ Security
Java Programming	Medical Assisting	Office Management
Jewelry	Medical Billing & Coding	Office Systems Technology

Oncology	Puppet Theater	Sports Exercise Psychology
Operations Management	Quality Control	Sports Management
Oracle	Race & Race Relations	Stained Glass
Organismic/ Evolutionary Biology	Radiation Therapy	Statistics
Orthodontics	Radiology	Strategy
Orthopedics	Real Estate	Supply Chain Management
Packaging	Recording Arts	Surgery
Painting	Recreation Management	Surgical Technology
Paper Making	Recreation/ Park Administration	Sustainability Studies
Paralegal Studies	Regional Studies	Sustainable Landscape Horticulture
Pathology	Regulatory Law	System Administration
Patient Care	Rehabilitation Therapy	Systems Development/Analyst
Pediatrics	Reiki	Technical Administration
Personal Training, Fitness	Religious & Spiritual Studies	Technical Management
Pharmacology	Research Methods	Technical Writing
Philosophy	Respiratory Care & Therapy	Technology in Education
Phlebotomy	Restaurant Management	Telecommunications
Photography	Robotics	Telecommunications Management
Physical Chemistry	Romance Languages & Literature	Theatre
Physical Education	Russian/East European Studies	Therapeutic Recreation
Physical Therapy	Sales	Tourism Studies
Physics	Sanskrit & Indian Studies	Toy Design
Physiology	School Leadership	Transplantation
Plant & Soil Science	Scientific Inquiry	Transportation Design
Plastic Surgery	Scientific Writing	Typography
Plumming	Sculpture	Ultrasound Technology
Poetry	Seamanship	United States Foreign Policy
Polarity	Silkscreen	Urban Education
Political Science	Small Business Management	Urban Planning & Design
Politics & Government	Social & Cultural History	Urban Studies
Population & International Health	Social Change	Vacations Management
Product Design	Social Medicine	Veterinary Animal Study
Production Operation Management	Social Policy	Visual & Environmental Studies
Project Management	Social Studies	Web Design/Development
Psychology	Social Work	Welding
Psychiatry	Sociology	Wildlife & Fisheries Biology
Public Administration	Software Development	Wine Studies
Public Health	Somatic Studies	Women's Studies
Public Policy/Public Service	Spa Therapies	Woodworking
Public Relations	Spanish	Yacht & Marine Design
Publishing	Speech Pathology	Zoology

Pinpointing areas that you are interested in studying is the first step toward directing your career. The next step is to take a class in the subject, read a book on the subject, interview someone already doing it, or try to find an internship with someone who works in this area. If this is something you may want to base a career on, do a little research first. You don't want to find after you graduate from college that you actually aren't interested in the jobs related to the subject you've been studying for the past four years.

Write any of the subjects that you starred on the previous page into the box below.

My most important subjects:

Now put your subjects in order, starting with the most important.
Check how meaningful each subject is to you. In what capacity do you want to learn the subject?
Here are some choices:

Mastery: know everything I can about this subject, become one of the top people in the field, or dedicate my life to this subject.

Career: have a job or career and be able to earn money through my knowledge of this subject.

College Major: graduate with a degree in this subject at an associate's, bachelor's, master's or doctorate level.

Take a class or two: just curious about the subject and may want to pursue it in the future, but not really sure what it's about, or want to have some knowledge of it.

Hobby: interested but don't need to take a class, or would rather study quietly on my own.

#1
- ☐ Mastery
- ☐ Career
- ☐ College major
- ☐ Take a class or two
- ☐ Hobby

#5
- ☐ Mastery
- ☐ Career
- ☐ College major
- ☐ Take a class or two
- ☐ Hobby

#2
- ☐ Mastery
- ☐ Career
- ☐ College major
- ☐ Take a class or two
- ☐ Hobby

#6
- ☐ Mastery
- ☐ Career
- ☐ College major
- ☐ Take a class or two
- ☐ Hobby

#3
- ☐ Mastery
- ☐ Career
- ☐ College major
- ☐ Take a class or two
- ☐ Hobby

#7
- ☐ Mastery
- ☐ Career
- ☐ College major
- ☐ Take a class or two
- ☐ Hobby

#4
- ☐ Mastery
- ☐ Career
- ☐ College major
- ☐ Take a class or two
- ☐ Hobby

#8
- ☐ Mastery
- ☐ Career
- ☐ College major
- ☐ Take a class or two
- ☐ Hobby

If you haven't included these subjects in your values, mission, vision, and steps for learning, go back and do this now. Maybe one of the subjects has such a strong calling that you want to incorporate it into your life vision as well or keep it in mind for the career chapter.

Any lingering thoughts or notes about what you want to know?

Five Years down the Road

In five years, I will be ___ years old. It will be the year 20___.
Here's what my life will look like:

Have you graduated from college? Have you entered the job market? Do you own your own business? Have you traveled the country or the world? Are you volunteering for the Peace Corps? Are you in the military? Are you married? Do you have kids? Do you live in your hometown? Your home state?

Picture what you want to be doing, and feel what it feels like to be you in five years. Do you feel different from how you are right now? Do you feel successful? Proud? Happy? Content with life?

Do you picture yourself doing something you don't want to be doing? Do you feel stuck? Unhappy? Out of options? What is it about your picture that brings up these feelings? Is there anything you can change in your current situation that would change your future? If this is where you are, first check out the roadblocks and detours in chapter 8.

Chapter 3

Need some time to sort all of this out?

Maybe you're feeling a little rushed to figure out your life. Maybe you still feel as though you have a lot more questions than answers. So...have you considered taking a little time to sort out your options for education or career?

Do you want to take some time off?

If **YES**, is this you?
❑ I need some time to think about where I want to go to college and what I want to study.

Or is this you?
❑ I have a good idea of what I want to do, but I'm not ready to start down this path just yet. I need a little time.

For either answer, you might consider taking a gap year to gain some new experience or learn more about your interests before choosing a college or career path. This chapter is **definitely** for you. You may still want to go through the application process for colleges if you know where you may want to go, but you can always defer your enrollment for a year until you are ready. It's usually easier while you are still in the school groove and surrounded by all the right people, to apply to some schools before you graduate.

Or is this you?
❑ I need some time to sort out my path, but I don't have any money.

In that case, it's time to get creative. Various organizations around the country offer volunteer experiences that include free housing. Some even pay you to participate. You can also apply for a Gap Year Scholarship to help you fund your year off (see page 54). Another option is to work for a little while, maybe just part-time, while you're figuring out school or career. Being in the workforce can give some useful perspective on what you want to do (or not do) for the rest of your life.

Or is this you?
❑ I would love to travel abroad, see new people and places, and improve my foreign language skills.

A gap year sounds perfect for you! You'll meet people all over the world who are taking time off to explore for months—even years—at a time. This chapter is definitely for you, and don't forget to look at the travel pages in chapter 7.

> **If none of these answers seem to fit, skim through this chapter to see if it interests you. You can always come back to it later.**

If **NO**, is this you?
❑ I know exactly what I want to do with my life, and I'm ready to get started.

Go for it! You can always take a year off down the road for an internship or travel. If it's not something that grabs your interest right now, move on to the next chapter.

Or is this you?
❑ Taking time off is a little scary because I might lose my momentum.

This is certainly a valid concern, especially from your parents' perspective. They might think that if you don't continue your schooling now, that you won't ever graduate. If it makes you (and them) feel better you can always apply to your college choices and defer enrollment for a semester or two. Don't worry, when you find a course of study that you are really interested in, you can get your momentum rolling again easily.

Or is this you?
❑ I would disappoint someone who cares about me if I didn't start school right away.

It comes down to this: who are you living your life for—yourself or someone else? Making a choice based on your fear of disappointing someone could very well end up disappointing someone who's even more important—that's right, YOU. Ultimately, the people who really care about us will support our decisions when we make them with the best intention to live a fulfilling life. Check out roadblocks and detours (chapter 8). Take a quick look at this chapter to see if anything piques your interest.

Or is this you?
❑ I already got accepted by my college of choice.

If you're ready for college, go for it! If you aren't ready, take some time to think about your path before you start accumulating all that debt. In the grand scheme of things, putting off your enrollment for a year isn't going to make you somehow "fall behind" in life. In a year's time you will have a much clearer sense of whether you're ready to pursue higher education.

What's a Gap Year?

The terms "gap year" and "year out" refer to a period of time off between high school and college, college and graduate school, or school and career.

Many people use this time to gain skills and practical "life experience" that you can't get in a classroom setting, by traveling, doing internships, or volunteering. Popular adventure programs like Outward Bound and National Outdoor Leadership School (NOLS) are another way to take a break from school while gaining valuable leadership, communication, and survival skills.

The reasons for taking a gap year are as varied as the people who take them. Some just need a year to "recharge their batteries". Others are ready to step out of their comfort zone by living and working or volunteering in a new and different environment, or they may just want to "try out" an occupation before committing themselves to years of study.

But what would colleges think?

You might think universities would try to discourage students from delaying enrollment or taking time off from their studies, but actually they *encourage* gap year options

"Fred Hargadon, former dean of admissions at Princeton University, said that the ideal age of an incoming freshman class would be over 21. He believed that they would then have the wisdom and experience to take full advantage of Princeton's offerings. Colleges are recognizing the obvious benefits of a freshman student who is more mature and focused, and less likely to drink to excess or flounder about changing majors."

Excerpt from "What Universities Say" at www.yearoutgroup.org.

But what would employers think?

Universities are not alone in their endorsement of a gap year. Employers are also starting to realize the benefits of hiring people who have had this experience.

"Becoming a ski instructor in Canada, teaching English in Cambodia or helping run summer camps in Russia...would make you more confident, a better leader, more worldly, more mature and to that end, a better employee. Most employers now, particularly the more progressive ones, would see all of those things as a great benefit."

Quoted from Campbell Sallabank CEO of career and networking site Linkme.com.au.

No single event in my life has affected me more, or more positively, than this course… It provided me with tools for teaching, and for living, that no textbook has or could ever offer. I cannot imagine the person who would not benefit from this experience.

——Outward Bound Participant
Excerpt from www.outwardbound.com

Consult the experts!

"Weeding out what is not of interest is as helpful as discovering what is. During my own gap year, I spent four months in Hawaii doing aquaculture research with visions of becoming a marine biologist. Within three weeks, I realized I had no patience for field research. This is not the kind of knowledge one can easily glean from a classroom setting.

On a personal level, these students have a better idea of who they are and what they can handle away from the familiarity of friends, family, and culture. They may have determined what kind of work they want to do in the world, or at least have a sense of work environments that may or may not suit them. On a practical level, they are building a resume before they hit college."

Holly Bull, president of the Center for Interim Programs Excerpt from "The Possibilities of the Gap Year," Chronicle of Higher Education 2006

Values and Choices for My Gap Year

If you are excited about this idea of taking a year to learn more about yourself, take a break from school, travel, or just try living on your own, this chapter will help you get clearer on what you would do during this time. The list below will just get you started, but there are hundreds of other values and choices for your gap year time. There is a more extensive list of gap year web sites and other gap year ideas on the links page at www.wheresthemap.com

What to do next? Go through the list of values.

 Check any that are important to you. ⭐ Star the really important ones.

❓ Question-mark any that make you go "Huh?" You can look those up later or just ignore them.

 If an important value is missing, write it in the margins.

	Where?		**How Long?**		Meeting new people
	Somewhere in my country		One month or less		Missionary/religious work
	In my state or region		Two to six months		Party!
	Africa		Six months to a year		Peace Corps
	Asia		One year or more		Recreation
	Australia		**What?**		Religious pilgrimage
	Europe		Adventure travel		Road trip
	North America		Agricultural work		Self-oriented
	South America		Beach time		Service oriented
	Pacific Islands		Building churches		Similar to future career
	National parks		Building homes		Sightseeing
	On a boat or ship		Building medical clinics		Social justice
	City		Building my résumé		Sports
	Small town or village		Building schools		Structured gap year program
	Rural area		Building villages		Work with indigenous cultures
	Developed country		Education		Vacation
	Developing country		Environmental education		Vocational training
	In the wilderness		Environmental work		Wilderness training
	World tour		Extreme Sports: SCUBA, Climbing		**With Whom?**
	When?		Figure out my career options		Family
	After high school		Figure out my life		Friends
	Before college or trade school		Free Time		Coworkers
	During college or trade school		Fun		On my own
	After college or trade school		Get my act together		People I meet while traveling
	Between degree programs		Get out of the house!		**How to Finance?**
	Before marriage		Government program		Pay my own way
	After marriage		Internship		Family
	Before starting a career		Leadership opportunity		Scholarship
	Sabbatical from a career		Learn or use a new language		Paid opportunity/stipend
	After retirement		Medical work		Work my way around the world

Write out any starred values or choices below.

Now put your values and choices in order, starting with the most important.

The most important values and choices for my gap year:

#1

#2

#3

#4

#5

#6

#7

#8

Gap Year Scholarship Program

Do you have big gap year dreams but a low gap year budget? If so, this is just what you've been looking for! Inspiration Publications is offering several one-thousand-dollar Gap Year Scholarships to readers of *Where's the Map? Create Your Own Guide to Life After Graduation*.

Scholarship Guidelines:
1. To be eligible for the scholarship you must be a citizen of the United States, have graduated from high school, and will be eighteen to twenty-five years old during your gap year experience.
2. Complete the Gap Year chapter in *Where's the Map? Create Your Own Guide to Life After Graduation* and type a two-page essay summarizing your values, mission, vision, and steps related to your proposed gap year experience. The essay should include where you want to go, what you want to do, why you want to do it, how you plan to get there, and how you plan to pay for the experience. Be sure to type your name and e-mail address in the upper right hand corner of each page.
3. Download the application form from our web site, fill it out on your computer as a PDF file and print it out.
4. If you're planning on doing an internship or working with a volunteer or travel organization, you also need to include proof of application/acceptance into the program.
5. Include one letter of recommendation from an adult in your life who can attest to your character and your desire, willingness, and ability to participate in your proposed gap year experience.
6. Applications will be awarded based on creativity, originality, clarity of your vision and passion to participate in your gap year opportunity.

See www.wheresthemap.com for more details about the scholarship and to download an application! We look forward to reading about your exciting plans!

Missions for My Gap Year

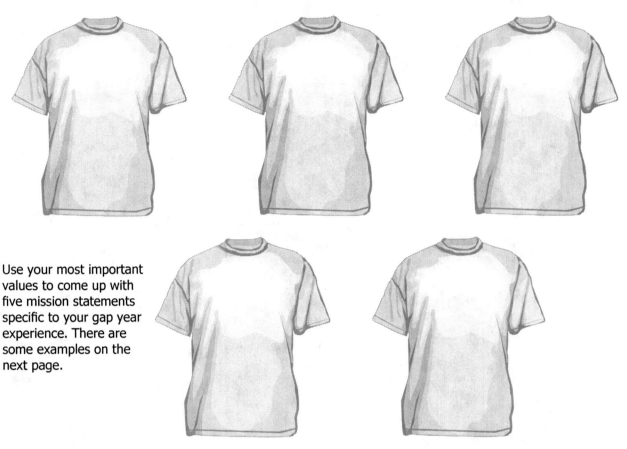

Use your most important values to come up with five mission statements specific to your gap year experience. There are some examples on the next page.

My Primary Mission:

From your smaller mission statements, write one primary mission for your gap year. Remember that the most important mission can represent your primary mission, or you can combine several statements.

If your mission or vision doesn't feel strong or clear, you may be forcing the idea of taking a gap year now. Go on to another chapter. And relax, these things don't have to be figured out overnight.

Here are a few mission and vision statements:

Meet people from all over the world.

Express my freedom!

Express my freedom

by moving to New York City and finding an apartment on my own.

Meet people from all over the world

by traveling through Europe and staying in hostels.

Sail in the Caribbean.

Gain some leadership experience.

Sail in the Caribbean

and relax "island style" on the money I make working on the boat.

Gain some leadership experience

in wilderness navigation and survival through a NOLS course.

Impress future employers.

Become fluent in Spanish.

Impress future employers

by taking an internship in marketing.

Become fluent in Spanish

while volunteering for three months in an orphanage in Mexico.

Vision for My Gap Year

Now that you've written your primary mission statement, create your primary vision statement. Remember, the vision statement shows the unique way that you see yourself accomplishing your mission. The vision can expand on what you want to do, what you will accomplish, what part of the country or world you want to be in, or how long you will spend. It should be specific and leave you feeling more focused.

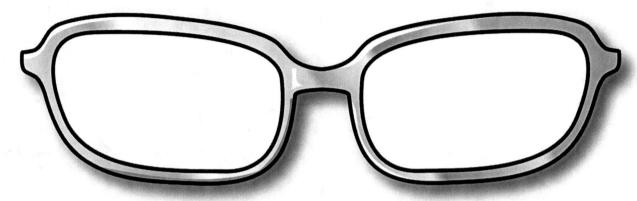

Jim's Story

My gap year in Washington was one of the most challenging and rewarding years of my life. I took the year after my master's degree to work with Habitat for Humanity as an Americorps volunteer. Americorps is like the Peace Corps, only you serve for one year within the United States instead of multiple years overseas. I worked with hundreds of people from all walks of life, from single moms on the waiting list for "Habitat Homes" to retired rocket scientists and corporate work teams from Microsoft. I also traveled to Georgia to participate in a "build-a-thon," where every Habitat Americorps group in the country came together to build fifty houses in a week. While there, we sat in on the Sunday School class taught by President Jimmy Carter at his home church! By far the most important and life-changing thing that happened during my gap year was meeting, dating, and eventually getting engaged to Beth. You never know what surprises will be waiting around the corner when you step out of your comfort zone and into the world!

I saw parts of Kenya I would never see as a typical tourist, but more importantly I actually gave something back to the local community. It was hard work but we became an equal in the community not just an outsider looking in. We didn't just come home with the odd souvenir and scenic photograph, we came back having built 4 dams from scratch, planted hundreds of trees and having helped some of the most deserving people have a better standard of living... an indescribable feeling!

Participant in Quest placement program who helped build dams, educate Akamba children, and plant trees.
Excerpt from Yearout.com

Exploring the Amazon jungle has always been an ambition of mine, but it's one of those things that you usually dream about rather than do. It was only when traveling up the Amazon River, surrounded by curious dolphins and overwhelmed by the resonating sounds of howler monkeys, that I realized my dream had come true. I was one of a 40-strong European team of young explorers working with experienced scientists from the University of Peru to carry out biodiversity studies to aid the ongoing battle to preserve the Amazon Jungle.

BSES Expeditions Participant
Excerpt from Yearout.com

Strategies for My Gap Year

Depending on your vision for your gap year, your strategies will vary. For this section, we've added some mission statements or slogans from a variety of organizations that offer gap programs, as well as some inspirational quotes that may help to guide your gap year experience.

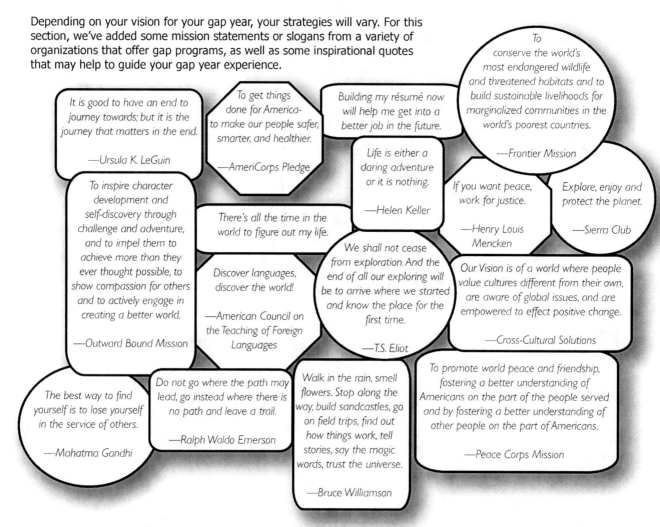

To conserve the world's most endangered wildlife and threatened habitats and to build sustainable livelihoods for marginalized communities in the world's poorest countries.
—Frontier Mission

It is good to have an end to journey towards; but it is the journey that matters in the end.
—Ursula K. LeGuin

To get things done for America- to make our people safer, smarter, and healthier.
—AmeriCorps Pledge

Building my résumé now will help me get into a better job in the future.

Life is either a daring adventure or it is nothing.
—Helen Keller

If you want peace, work for justice.
—Henry Louis Mencken

Explore, enjoy and protect the planet.
—Sierra Club

To inspire character development and self-discovery through challenge and adventure, and to impel them to achieve more than they ever thought possible, to show compassion for others and to actively engage in creating a better world.
—Outward Bound Mission

There's all the time in the world to figure out my life.

Discover languages, discover the world!
—American Council on the Teaching of Foreign Languages

We shall not cease from exploration. And the end of all our exploring will be to arrive where we started and know the place for the first time.
—T.S. Eliot

Our Vision is of a world where people value cultures different from their own, are aware of global issues, and are empowered to effect positive change.
—Cross-Cultural Solutions

The best way to find yourself is to lose yourself in the service of others.
—Mahatma Gandhi

Do not go where the path may lead, go instead where there is no path and leave a trail.
—Ralph Waldo Emerson

Walk in the rain, smell flowers. Stop along the way, build sandcastles, go on field trips, find out how things work, tell stories, say the magic words, trust the universe.
—Bruce Williamson

To promote world peace and friendship, fostering a better understanding of Americans on the part of the people served and by fostering a better understanding of other people on the part of Americans.
—Peace Corps Mission

Star any of the strategies, quotes, or mission statements above that inspire you. Maybe you even want to alter your own vision statement to reflect some of the ideas above. Are there any new strategies that you want to incorporate into your gap year planning? Write these in below:

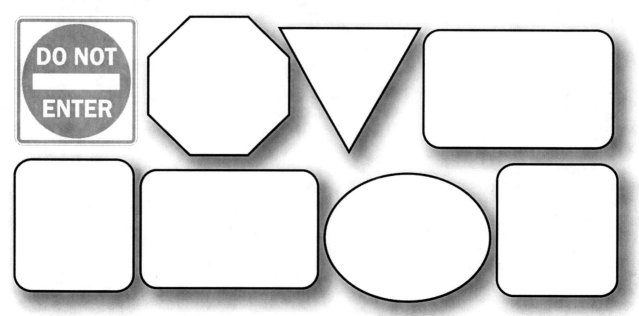

Steps for My Gap Year

Now's the time for you to map out any steps that will help you pursue your vision for taking some time off. Remember to base your steps on the primary vision statement you created on the last page.

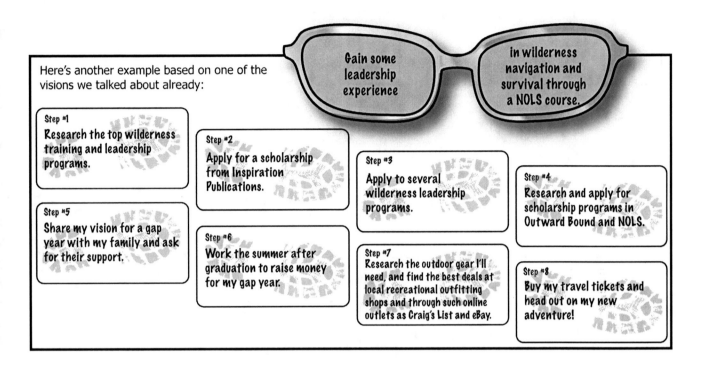

Here's another example based on one of the visions we talked about already:

Gain some leadership experience **in wilderness navigation and survival through a NOLS course.**

Step #1
Research the top wilderness training and leadership programs.

Step #2
Apply for a scholarship from Inspiration Publications.

Step #3
Apply to several wilderness leadership programs.

Step #4
Research and apply for scholarship programs in Outward Bound and NOLS.

Step #5
Share my vision for a gap year with my family and ask for their support.

Step #6
Work the summer after graduation to raise money for my gap year.

Step #7
Research the outdoor gear I'll need, and find the best deals at local recreational outfitting shops and through such online outlets as Craig's List and eBay.

Step #8
Buy my travel tickets and head out on my new adventure!

The adventure of life is to learn.
The goal of life is to grow.

—Arthur Ward

Step #1

Step #2

Step #3

Step #4

Step #5

Step #6

Step #7

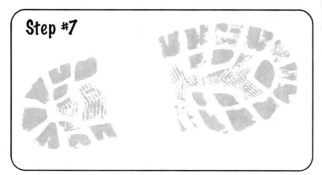

Step #8

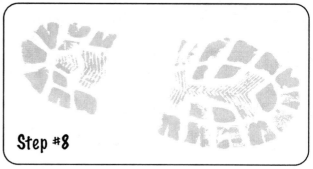

Step #9

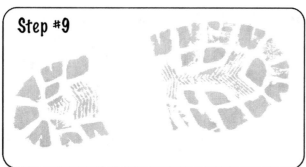

Step #10

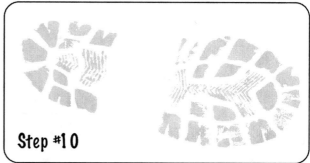

Step #11

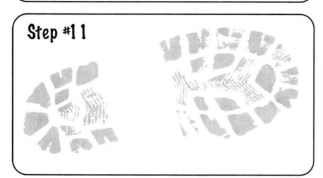

Step #12

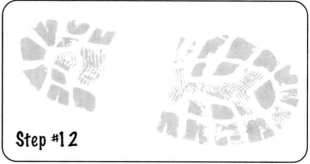

Step #13

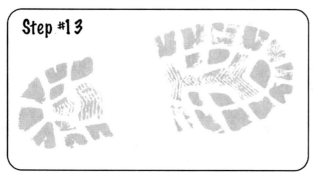

Step #14

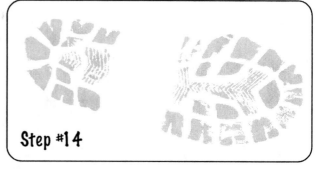

Any lingering thoughts or notes about taking some time off?

*At the center
of your being you
have the answer.*

*You know who you
are and you know
what you want.*

—Lao Tzu

Chapter 4

How do you want to make a living?

Chances are, you're going to spend a good chunk of your life working because you need to provide for your basic needs of shelter, clothing, and sustenance, not to mention all the other ways you may choose to spend money. So consider this: if so much of your time goes into making a living, why not do something you really enjoy? Someone has to pilot jet airplanes, design video games, play cello in the Boston Philharmonic, build Mars landing modules, star in major motion pictures, or be a taste-tester at Ben and Jerry's, so it might as well be you! Let's see where you are:

Do you know what you want to do to make a living?

If **YES**, is this you?
❑ I know the career I want and the path to get me there.

You may be able to skip this chapter altogether, but it may serve you to create a mission and vision to keep you on track. Double-check that your skills, values, and preferences are in line with your career choice.

Or is this you?
❑ I have a good idea what I want to do, but I haven't the foggiest notion how to get there.

You may skip the skills and careers list, or you could stop there briefly to see if any other occupations interest you. Definitely go through the values section, and spend some extra time on the steps. Doing some research and simply talking to other people in your area of choice will probably be the most helpful.

Or is this you?
❑ I have a career planned, but it's not something I'm really looking forward to.

Stop! Take your time to make this decision. Go through this chapter and get clearer on what you care about and what you value. Look at your reasons for choosing a particular path. Do they fit with your primary mission and vision?

Or is this you?
❑ I have a job lined up after high school, and I don't care about having a career in something I'm interested in. I just need to pay the bills.

Skip this chapter entirely, and try out one of the later ones, say, chapter 5, 6, or 7. We probably won't change your mind at this stage, but consider looking at your skills and interests to see if there's a job you can at least tolerate—and maybe even enjoy.

If none of these answers seem to fit, skim through this chapter to see if it interests you. You can always come back to it later.

If **NO**, is this you?
❑ I'm not ready yet to think about a career.
❑ A lot of career areas look interesting, but I don't know which one to pursue.

For either answer, you might consider taking a gap year to gain some new experience or learn more about your interests before choosing a career path. If you haven't already done so, turn to chapter 3 and explore your options of a gap year. Go through the career chapter anyway to identify your strongest values, skills, interests, and preferences.

Or is this you?
❑ I can't imagine doing just one thing for the rest of my life!

This is certainly a valid thought. Your vision will evolve over time, and your interests will change, so you may have more than one career in your lifetime. If you can't imagine having one career right now, it sounds as though you haven't found your vision. Use the values section to help you create a vision for career, and if your life vision is still a little shaky, revisit chapter 1.

Or is this you?
❑ I don't even know what I would be good at.

Start with "What's my thing?" and see if you can identify any skills or talents that you could turn into a career. Try asking some friends, teachers, or family members if they have any ideas to help with these exercises.

Or is this you?
❑ I don't want to define myself by my career when there is so much more to life.

You're right—some people focus so much on who they are in their career that they miss out on the bigger picture of who they *really* are. You don't need a career vision if you have a clearly laid-out life vision. Revisit chapter 1 and check out some of the later chapters to see if they speak to you more.

What's My Thing?

It's easy to overlook the things you're good at, because they seem so normal to you. But even the simplest skills are not everyone's forte. Do you really think everyone is good at fixing cars? Or is a good listener? Or can design web sites in their sleep? What makes you "you"?

To get you started in uncovering your skills, take a look at the questions below. Star anything that you might like to do for a living.

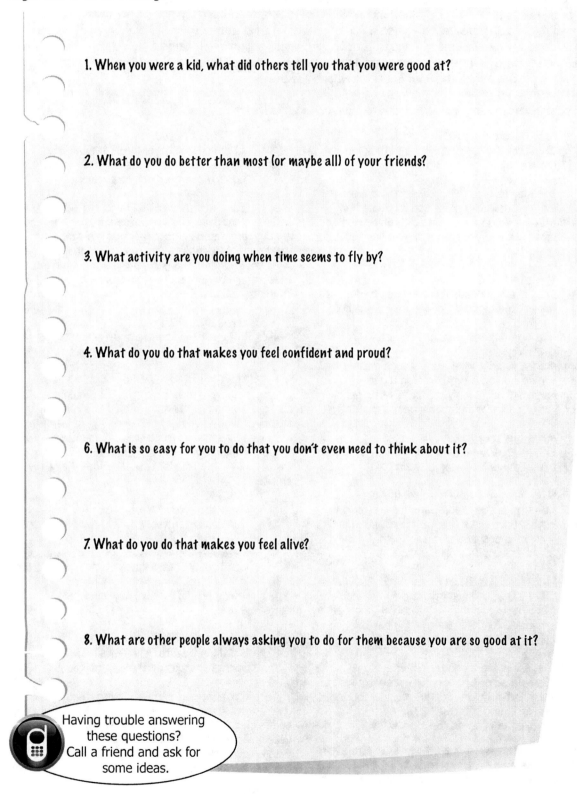

1. When you were a kid, what did others tell you that you were good at?

2. What do you do better than most (or maybe all) of your friends?

3. What activity are you doing when time seems to fly by?

4. What do you do that makes you feel confident and proud?

6. What is so easy for you to do that you don't even need to think about it?

7. What do you do that makes you feel alive?

8. What are other people always asking you to do for them because you are so good at it?

Having trouble answering these questions? Call a friend and ask for some ideas.

My Skills & Talents

List #1. Check any of the actions below that you could say: *I am good at* _____.
If you also enjoy the action and would consider making a living from it, give it a star.

	Accomplishing		Designing		Influencing		Promoting
	Achieving		Determining		Inspecting		Proposing
	Acquiring		Developing		Inspiring		Providing
	Adapting		Devising		Installing		Publishing
	Administering		Directing		Interacting		Questioning
	Advising		Dispensing		Interpreting		Reading
	Analyzing		Displaying		Interviewing		Re-arranging
	Assembling		Distributing		Inventing		Receiving
	Assisting		Documenting		Investing		Recommending
	Baking		Drafting		Investigating		Record keeping
	Budgeting		Dramatizing		Joining		Recording
	Building		Driving		Keeping		Rehabilitating
	Buying		Earning		Learning		Relating
	Calculating		Editing		Leasing		Remembering
	Changing		Empowering		Listening		Repairing
	Checking		Encouraging		Locating		Reporting
	Clarifying		Endorsing		Maintaining		Representing
	Classifying		Enduring		Making		Researching
	Coaching		Enforcing		Managing		Resolving
	Collaborating		Entertaining		Measuring		Running
	Collecting		Establishing		Mediating		Saving
	Comparing		Estimating		Meeting		Screening
	Competing		Evaluating		Memorizing		Selling
	Compiling		Examining		Monitoring		Serving
	Completing		Explaining		Motivating		Sketching
	Composing		Exploring		Moving		Solving
	Comprehending		Expressing		Negotiating		Speaking
	Conducting		Facilitating		Observing		Starting
	Confronting		Finding		Opening		Succeeding
	Constructing		Filing		Operating		Summarizing
	Converting		Fixing		Organizing		Supervising
	Coordinating		Gardening		Overseeing		Supporting
	Coping		Gathering		Owning		Teaching
	Corresponding		Generating		Participating		Thinking
	Counseling		Giving		Performing		Timing
	Creating		Granting		Persevering		Tolerating
	Deciding		Guiding		Persuading		Translating
	Decorating		Handling		Picking out		Troubleshooting
	Defining		Helping		Planning		Typing
	Delegating		Identifying		Playing		Uncovering
	Delivering		Imagining		Predicting		Understanding
	Demonstrating		Implementing		Preparing		Updating
	Describing		Improving		Programming		Writing

My Identity

List #2: Check any of the words below that describe you or how you work. Star the qualities that you would most like to use in making a living.

Accepting	Deliberate	Imaginative	Permissive	Serious
Adaptable	Demanding	Impatient	Persevering	Service-oriented
Adventurous	Dependable	Impersonal	Persistent	Sharing
Affirming	Dependent	Impulsive	Persuasive	Sharp-tongued
Aggressive	Determined	In-charge	Pessimistic	Shrewd
Aloof	Devoted	Inclusive	Playful	Shy
Ambitious	Diligent	Inconsistent	Polished	Simple
Amiable	Diplomatic	Independent	Polite	Sincere
Argumentative	Direct	Innovative	Popular	Smooth
Arrogant	Disciplined	Inquisitive	Positive	Social
Articulate	Down-to-earth	Insightful	Practical	Sophisticated
Artistic	Easygoing	Intellectual	Pragmatic	Spontaneous
Assertive	Efficient	Intense	Private	Steady
Bold	Emotional	Interactive	Problem-solving	Strategic
Born to lead	Empathetic	Intimate	Punctual	Strong
Bossy	Energetic	Intimidating	Questioning	Stubborn
Calm	Enthusiastic	Introspective	Quiet	Supportive
Caring	Entrepreneurial	Inventive	Realistic	Suspicious
Cautious	Expeditious	Kindly	Rebellious	Sympathetic
Chaotic	Experimenting	Laid-back	Relaxed	Systematic
Cheerful	Expressive	Liberal	Reliable	Tactful
Clever	Fearless	Lively	Reserved	Tactile
Clingy	Flexible	Loyal	Respectful	Take charge
Compassionate	Focused	Modest	Responsible	Tenacious
Competitive	Forthright	Moralistic	Responsive	Tenderhearted
Concerned	Fun-loving	Multifaceted	Restrained	Tense
Conforming	Generous	Noncompetitive	Rigid	Thorough
Confrontational	Gentle	Nurturing	Robust	Tolerant
Congenial	Genuine	Obedient	Sarcastic	Tough-minded
Conservative	Giving	Objective	Self-centered	Traditional
Consistent	Global-thinking	Observant	Self-confident	Trusting
Controlling	Goal-oriented	Open	Self-critical	Tyrannical
Cool	Gracious	Optimistic	Self-determined	Unbendable
Cooperative	Gregarious	Orderly	Self-effacing	Uncomplicated
Cordial	Hardworking	Organized	Self-indulgent	Unsentimental
Creative	Harmonious	Original	Self-sacrificing	Versatile
Critical	Helpful	Outgoing	Self-sufficient	Virtuous
Daydreaming	Holistic	Patient	Sensitive	Vivacious
Decisive	Humorous	Peace-loving	Sentimental	Warm
Deep	Idealistic	Perceptive	Serene	Witty

#3. Write anything that you starred on the last three pages into the box below.

My most important talents, traits, gifts, skills, or qualities:

Using what you wrote above, think about how you would complete the following sentence:

I am good at _____   _____ for/to/with/by/in _____.
　　　　　　　(Fill in the action)　　　(Fill in a Person, Place, or Thing)　　　　　　(Fill in another noun or verb)

Example: *I am good at handling complaints from customers.*

Now, on the next page craft a few statements like the example above which highlight your favorite skills. Think about how meaningful each skill is to you and how you would like to incorporate it into your vision. To what level do you want to master these skills? Here are some choices:

Mastery: to be a master of this skill, to be able to do it in my sleep, to become known as one of the top people using this skill, or to dedicate my life to it.

Career: to have a job or career and be able to earn money with this skill.

College Major: to graduate with a degree that teaches or uses this skill at an associate's, bachelor's, master's or doctorate level.

Take a class or two: just interested in getting better at this skill and may want to pursue it someday.

Hobby: interested, but don't need to take a class, or would rather practice it quietly on my own.

A few ideas for people, places, and things to complete your statement:

Animals	Goals	Operations
Art	Healthcare	Plants
Body	Houses	Problems
Buildings	Ideas	Products
Cars	Individuals	Programs
Children	Information	Quality
Conflicts	Instruments	Reports
Crowds	Interviews	Rules
Data	Knowledge	Schedules
Details	Land	Solutions
Entertainment	Languages	Tasks
Executives	Meetings	Teams
Feelings	Money	Time
Food	Offices	Tools

Examples:

I am good at <u>teaching kids</u> how to <u>read</u>.

- ❏ Mastery!
- ☑ Career
- ❏ College major
- ❏ Take a class or two
- ❏ Hobby

I am good at <u>performing stand-up comedy in front of a crowd</u>.

- ❏ Mastery!
- ❏ Career
- ❏ College major
- ❏ Take a class or two
- ☑ Hobby

#1

- ❏ Mastery!
- ❏ Career
- ❏ College major
- ❏ Take a class or two
- ❏ Hobby

#2

- ❏ Mastery!
- ❏ Career
- ❏ College major
- ❏ Take a class or two
- ❏ Hobby

#3

- ❏ Mastery!
- ❏ Career
- ❏ College major
- ❏ Take a class or two
- ❏ Hobby

#4

- ❏ Mastery!
- ❏ Career
- ❏ College major
- ❏ Take a class or two
- ❏ Hobby

#5

- ❏ Mastery!
- ❏ Career
- ❏ College major
- ❏ Take a class or two
- ❏ Hobby

#6

- ❏ Mastery!
- ❏ Career
- ❏ College major
- ❏ Take a class or two
- ❏ Hobby

#7

- ❏ Mastery!
- ❏ Career
- ❏ College major
- ❏ Take a class or two
- ❏ Hobby

#8

- ❏ Mastery!
- ❏ Career
- ❏ College major
- ❏ Take a class or two
- ❏ Hobby

Are you more concerned about making a ton of money or having a job that's interesting or exciting? Maybe both? Which is more important: being able to spend time with your family or having big responsibility at work? Would you rather work in a natural outdoor setting, or wear a suit and tie and work in an office?

Once again, the life values you identified in chapter 1 may be helpful in determining your career values and preferences. Revisit them now and write any that you think would be appropriate in the margins below. The following table lists some values and choices that may help you narrow down what is most important for you in a work environment.

What to do next? Go through the list of values.

✓ Check any that are important to you. ★ Star the really important ones.

? Question-mark any that make you go "Huh?" You can look those up later or just ignore them.

 If an important value is missing, write it in the margins.

The basics	Nonoffice setting	White-collar job
Job right after high school	Private office	Long-term job security
Career after college	Cubicle	Freedom more important than security
One career for life	Get hands dirty	Competitive environment
Changing careers over lifetime	No dirt please!	Cooperative environment
Work can be fun	**The job itself**	Competition within your workplace
Work is never fun	College education required	Competition with other companies
Logistics	High school education required	Highly competitive field
Urban	Variety of different tasks	Easily hired with little competition
Rural	Basically the same task every day	Rapidly expanding field
Suburban	Rewarded for overtime	Slow and steady growth
Big city	No pressure to put in any overtime	**The workday**
Small city	Government job	Fast-paced workplace
Frequent travel	Nongovernment job	Slower-paced workplace
Occasional travel	Self-employed	Many meetings a day
International travel	Paycheck comes from someone else!	Very rarely do I need a meeting
Domestic travel	Work in educational system	Speaking in front of people
Local travel	Service industry	No public speaking
Never leave home	Manufacturing industry	Use my body mostly
Potential to transfer to new locations	High tech industry	Use my mind mostly
Job specific to one area only	Work for salary	Physical labor
Commute to work	Work by the hour	Not too exerting
Work within ten minutes of home	Non-profit organization	Related to an interesting subject
Work from my home	Big corporation	Work doesn't need to be interesting
Work outside my home	Midsized company	Challenging work
Work inside	Small business	Very little thinking involved
Work outside	Start-up company	Formal workplace
Natural setting	Well-established company	Relaxed workplace
Nature scares me!	Forty-hour workweek or less	Keep my own schedule
Working at a desk all day	Between forty- and sixty-hours	Punch a clock
Work that keeps me on the move	Sixty-plus-hous workweek	Bring work home
Work in an office	Blue-collar job	Work stays at the office

Night shift	Manage over a hundred employees	Work with the poor
Day shift	Opportunity for advancement	Work with the rich
Flexible schedule	Upper management	Work with employees
Set schedule	Lower management	Work with customers
Dress code	Receiving great respect from others	Teamwork important
Wear whatever I want	Respect not necessary	Individual effort more important
Dressy - suit and tie all the way	Using my full potential	**Benefits!**
Casual within reason	**The people**	Public recognition and praise
Constant decision making	Close personal friendships at work	Save the kudos--just pay me
Seldom need to make decisions	No friendships at work	Benefits important
Slow and deliberate decision making	Constantly working with people	Benefits not so important
Fast-paced, high-pressure job	Keep to myself most of the day	Two weeks of vacation
I know what I'll be doing every day	Lots of interaction, face-to-face contact	More vacation please!
New projects nearly every day	Contact by phone or e-mail only	Maternity leave
Plenty of time to spend with family	Interact directly with under five people	Set my own vacations
Not much time for family life	Interact directly with over fifty people	Workplace sets my vacation
Heavy responsibility	Limited interaction with management	Retire at sixty-five
No responsibility	Constant interaction with manager	Pension plan
The position	Work with children	A career I can still do when I'm eighty
Job of my dreams is essential	Work with young adults	Work until I die
A job is just a job	Work with adults	Early retirement
Management position	Work with seniors	Enough money for all my needs
Employee position	Work in my own country	More money than I could ever need
Manage fewer than five employees	Work abroad	Making a contribution to society

Write out any starred values or preferences below.

The most important values and choices for my career:

Now put your values and choices in order, starting with the most important.

#1

#2

#3

#4

#5

#6

#7

#8

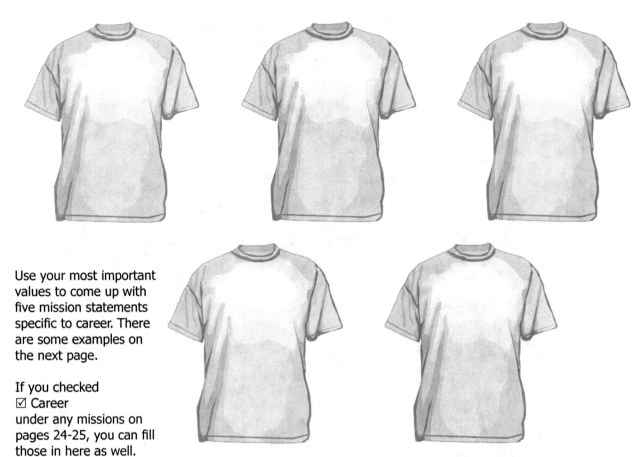

Use your most important values to come up with five mission statements specific to career. There are some examples on the next page.

If you checked
☑ Career
under any missions on pages 24-25, you can fill those in here as well.

My Primary Mission:

From your smaller mission statements, write one primary mission for your career. Remember, that you can use the most important as your primary mission, or you can combine several.

If your mission or vision doesn't feel very strong or clear, you may just need a little more time to sort out what your focus is for your career.

Here are a few mission and vision statements:

Be a professional violinist.

Get a job, any job.

Get a job, any job

that will allow me to pay the bills, support my family, and have weekends off.

Be a professional violinist

and play with the Boston Philharmonic.

Work as a high school science teacher.

Be my own boss.

Work as a high school science teacher

and inspire my students to protect the environment.

Be my own boss

by running my own fashion boutique in Los Angeles.

Have a successful career in the military.

Beecome a high-level executive.

Have a successful career in the military

and attain the rank of full colonel.

Become a high-level executive

in a Fortune 500 company and make $500,000 a year.

Vision for My Career

Now that you have your primary mission statement, create your primary vision statement. Remember, the vision statement shows the unique way that you see yourself accomplishing your mission. The vision could expand on where you want to work, what sort of people you want to work with, what part of the country or the world you want to be in, how fast you want to be promoted, or how much money you want to make. It should get more specific and leave you feeling more focused.

Are you looking for more guidance in choosing a great career? Check out the Rockport Institute, an international career counseling network. The founder, Nicholas Lore, wrote a very thorough and enlightening book on the subject, called *The Pathfinder*. This book was instrumental in guiding us to the career path we are on now.

Roadtrip Nation

Here's a story about some guys we really resonated with. With college graduation fast approaching, Mike Marriner, Brian McAllister, and Nathan Gebhard realized they were all staring down the gun barrel of lives they were not especially thrilled about, and they began to wonder if there might be another way. They decided to exit from the metaphorical freeway they were on—you know, the one leading to mundane careers and dull, passionless lives—so they literally hit the road in an old green RV in search of people who had truly found their calling. During their seventeen-thousand-mile adventure, they met people who were living their vision: the executive director of Greenpeace, the creator/producer of the TV shows *Survivor* and *The Apprentice*, and the editor of *Seventeen* magazine, among many others. What started out as a three-month road trip has evolved into three books, an active online community, and a PBS TV series called *Roadtrip Nation*. Every summer they select new teams of students to take to the road in a green RV, in search of inspiring people.

For more information about the Rockport Institue, *Roadtrip Nation*, or Living Land and Waters, visit WheresTheMap.com.

Friend of a Friend Story

Turning a Vision into a Living

The Mississippi River was literally Chad Pregracke's backyard when he was growing up. While in high school and college, he spent his summers working as a fisherman, shell diver, and barge hand for a number of commercial operations. Appalled at the amount of garbage that he saw accumulating in and along our great rivers, he decided to spearhead a cleanup operation. After years of trying unsuccessfully to get government assistance for his efforts, he decided to form Living Lands and Waters, a not-for-profit organization based in East Moline, Illinois, and seek private sponsorship of his river projects. To date, with the help of thousands of volunteers and millions of dollars in donations, LL&W has pulled over four million pounds of garbage from, and implemented river bottom and shoreline restoration projects in and along, almost all of America's major rivers. Chad has not only turned his love of the river into a fulfilling life's work, but his efforts have also earned him international recognition and inspired a new movement to help preserve our precious river ecosystems. Recruitment of new volunteers and donors is an ongoing effort. To learn more, check out Chad's book, *From the Bottom Up: One Man's Crusade to Clean America's Rivers*.

Strategies for My Career

People's opinions on work and career run the gamut. Some see work as drudgery, while others see it as an expression of their life's passion and a doorway to their dreams. You may have grown up with parents who hated their jobs while feeling at the same time that they could not leave them, so their strategy may have been, "Work is something you have to do; it was never meant to be enjoyable." On the other hand, if you know someone who has a career that they love and look forward to every day, you may have learned the strategy "Work can be fun and satisfying."

Below are some quotes about working that represent a number of different perspectives that can be turned into strategies. Which ones are you most familiar with? Which ones do you believe? Remember, you can change your strategies, but you will typically need to develop a real sense that they are true for you.

Work is never done.

Work for something because it is good, not just because it stands a chance to succeed.
——Vaclav Havel

What we really want to do is what we are really meant to do. When we do what we are meant to do, money comes to us, doors open for us, we feel useful, and the work we do feels like play to us.
—Julia Cameron

Genius is one percent inspiration and ninety-nine percent perspiration.
—Thomas Edison

I believe you are your work. Don't trade the stuff of your life, time, for nothing more than dollars.
—Rita Mae Brown

Find something you love to do and you'll never have to work a day in your life.
—Harvey MacKay

Work spares us from three evils: boredom, vice, and need.
——Voltaire

Work is either fun or drudgery. It depends on your attitude.
—Colleen C. Barrett

It's important to know that words don't move mountains. Work, exacting work moves mountains.
—Danilo Dolci

Never work just for money or for power. They won't save your soul or help you sleep at night.
—Marian Wright Edelman

Happiness is an attitude. We either make ourselves miserable, or happy and strong. The amount of work is the same.
-Francesca Reigler

Always be smarter than the people who hire you.
—Lena Horne

The secret of joy in work is contained in one word - excellence. To know how to do something well is to enjoy it.
—Pearl S. Buck

Hard work is the price we must pay for success.

The true way to render ourselves happy is to love our work and find in it our pleasure.
——Francoise de Motteville

We work to become, not to acquire.
—Elbert Hubbard

You get out of it only what you put into it.

Star any strategies above that are line with your values, your mission and your vision for working. Fill in any other useful work strategies which will help support your vision for career.

Steps for My Career

Now's the time for you to map out whatever steps will help you pursue your career vision. Remember to base your steps on the primary vision statement you created on the previous page.

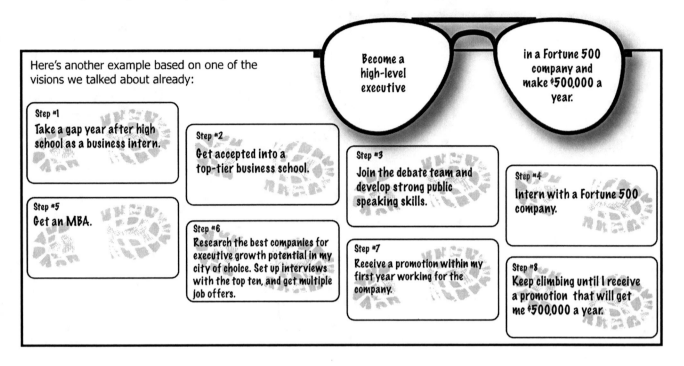

Here's another example based on one of the visions we talked about already:

Become a high-level executive **in a Fortune 500 company and make $500,000 a year.**

Step #1
Take a gap year after high school as a business intern.

Step #2
Get accepted into a top-tier business school.

Step #3
Join the debate team and develop strong public speaking skills.

Step #4
Intern with a Fortune 500 company.

Step #5
Get an MBA.

Step #6
Research the best companies for executive growth potential in my city of choice. Set up interviews with the top ten, and get multiple job offers.

Step #7
Receive a promotion within my first year working for the company.

Step #8
Keep climbing until I receive a promotion that will get me $500,000 a year.

To accomplish great things, we must not only act, but also dream; not only plan, but also believe.

—Anatole France

Step #1

Step #2

Step #3

Step #4

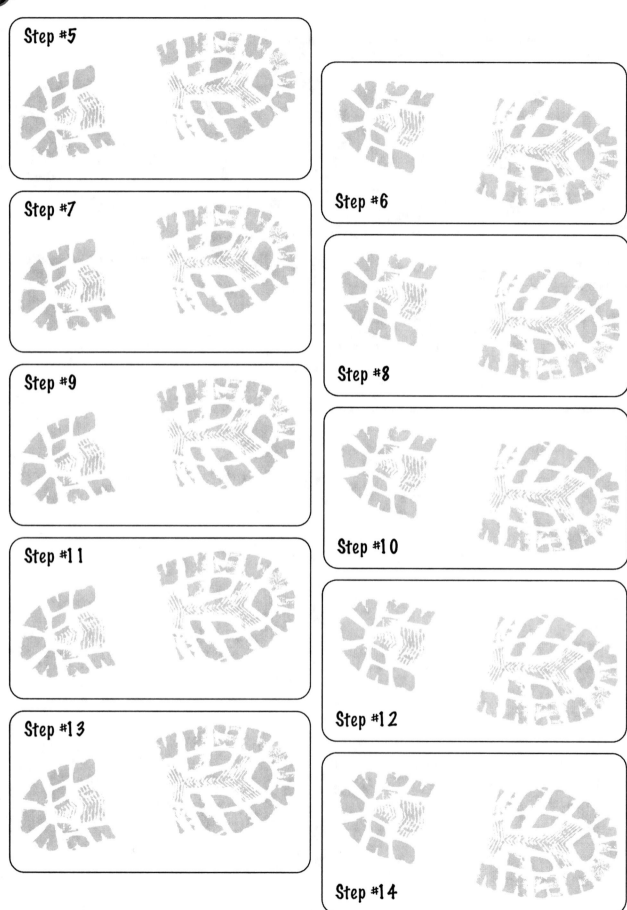

Step #5

Step #6

Step #7

Step #8

Step #9

Step #10

Step #11

Step #12

Step #13

Step #14

So Many Jobs, So Little Time

There are an infinite number of ways to make a living. Below is a list of occupations recognized by the U.S. Department of Labor. This list is a good starting point to see what some of your options are—but remember, it still only scratches the surface of what's available out there.

For a list of nearly every type of business available, check out the Yellow Pages. If you're mainly looking for ideas of what is available in your community, use a local phone book. If you want a broader field of information, your local library will most likely have copies of the phone books for all major cities in your region. Or, to get the most information the fastest (or if you just don't like flipping through those big books and getting that funny-smelling ink all over your hands), check out the Yellow Pages online where you will find businesses listed by category, for every city in the United States and Canada. Go to www. wheresthemap.com to access this directory.

What to do next? Go through the list of possible careers.

✔ Check any that are look interesting.   ★ Star the ones that seem the best match for you.

❓ Question-mark any that you are not sure about.   ✖ Cross out any that make you cringe.

✎ Write in any interesting careers that you don't see.

Professional and related occupations	Physicists and astronomers
Computer and mathematical occupations	**Social scientists and related occupations**
Actuaries	Economists
Computer programmers	Market and survey researchers
Computer scientists and database administrators	Psychologists
Computer software engineers	Urban and regional planners
Computer support specialists and systems administrators	Social scientists
Computer systems analysts	Science technicians
Mathematicians	**Community and social services occupations**
Operations research analysts	Counselors
Statisticians	Probational officers and correctional treatment specialists
Architects, surveyors, and cartographers	Social and human service assistants
Architects, except landscape and naval	Social workers
Landscape architects	**Legal occupations**
Surveyors, cartographers, photogrammetrists, and surveying	Court reporters
Engineers	Judges, magistrates, and other judicial workers
Drafters and engineering technicians	Lawyers
Drafters	Paralegals and legal assistants
Engineering technicians	**Education, training, library, and museum occupations**
Life scientists	Archivists, curators, and museum technicians
Agricultural and food scientists	Instructional coordinators
Biological scientists	Librarians
Conservation scientists and foresters	Library technicians
Medical scientists	Teacher assistants
Physical scientists	Teachers—adult literacy and remedial education
Atmospheric scientists	Teachers—postsecondary
Chemists and materials scientists	Teachers—preschool, kindergarten, elementary, middle, secondary
Environmental scientists and hydrologists	Teachers—self-enrichment education
Geoscientists	Teachers—special education

Art and design occupations	Emergency medical technicians and paramedics
Artists and related workers	Licensed practical and licensed vocational nurses
Commercial and industrial designers	Medical records and health information technicians
Fashion designers	Nuclear medicine technologists
Floral designers	Occupational health and safety specialists and technicians
Graphic designers	Opticians, dispensing
Interior designers	Pharmacy technicians
Entertainers, performers & sports occupations	Radiologic technologists and technicians
Actors, producers, and directors	Surgical technologists
Athletes, coaches, umpires, and related workers	Veterinary technologists and technicians
Dancers and choreographers	**Service occupations**
Musicians, singers, and related workers	**Healthcare support occupations**
Media and communications-related occupations	Dental assistants
Announcers	Massage therapists
Broadcast and sound engineering technicians and radio operators	Medical assistants
Interpreters and translators	Medical transcriptionists
News analysts, reporters, and correspondents	Nursing, psychiatric, and home health aides
Photographers	Occupational therapist assistants and aides
Public relations specialists	Pharmacy aides
Television, video, and motion picture camera operators and editors	Physical therapist assistants and aides
Writers and editors	**Protective service occupations**
Health diagnosing and treating occupations	Correctional officers
Audiologists	Fire fighting occupations
Chiropractors	Police and detectives
Dentists	Private detectives and investigators
Dietitians and nutritionists	Security guards and gaming surveillance officers
Occupational therapists	**Food preparation and serving related occupations**
Optometrists	Chefs, cooks, and food preparation workers
Pharmacists	Food and beverage serving and related workers
Physical therapists	**Cleaning & maintenance occupations**
Physician assistants	Building cleaning workers
Physicians and surgeons	Grounds maintenance workers
Podiatrists	Pest control workers
Radiation therapists	**Personal care and service occupations**
Recreational therapists	Animal care and service workers
Registered nurses	Barbers, cosmetologists, and other personal appearance workers
Respiratory therapists	Childcare workers
Speech-language pathologists	Fitness workers
Veterinarians	Flight attendants
Health technologists and technicians	Gaming services occupations
Athletic trainers	Personal and home care aides
Cardiovascular technologists and technicians	Recreation workers
Clinical laboratory technologists and technicians	**Management occupations**
Dental hygienists	Administrative services managers
Diagnostic medical sonographers	Advertising, marketing, promotions, public relations, & sales manag-

Computer and information systems managers	Gaming cage workers
Construction managers	Payroll and timekeeping clerks
Education administrators	Procurement clerks
Engineering and natural sciences managers	Tellers
Farmers, ranchers, and agricultural managers	***Information and record clerks***
Financial managers	Brokerage clerks
Food service managers	Credit authorizers, checkers, and clerks
Funeral directors	Customer service representatives
Human resources, training, & labor relations managers & specialists	File clerks
Industrial production managers	Hotel, motel, and resort desk clerks
Lodging managers	Human resources assistants, except payroll and timekeeping
Medical and health services managers	Interviewers
Property, real estate, and community association managers	Library assistants, clerical
Purchasing managers, buyers, and purchasing agents	Order clerks
Top executives	Receptionists and information clerks
Business and financial operations occupations	Reservation and transportation ticket agents and travel clerks
Accountants and auditors	***Material recording & distributing occupations***
Appraisers and assessors of real estate	Cargo and freight agents
Budget analysts	Couriers and messengers
Claims adjusters, appraisers, examiners, and investigators	Dispatchers
Cost estimators	Meter readers, utilities
Financial analysts and personal financial advisors	Postal Service workers
Insurance underwriters	Production, planning, and expediting clerks
Loan officers	Shipping, receiving, and traffic clerks
Management analysts	Stock clerks and order fillers
Meeting and convention planners	Weighers, measurers, checkers, and samplers, record keeping
Tax examiners, collectors, and revenue agents	***Other office and administrative support occupations***
Sales and related occupations	Communications equipment operators
Advertising sales agents	Computer operators
Cashiers	Data entry and information processing workers
Counter and rental clerks	Desktop publishers
Demonstrators, product promoters, and models	Office and administrative support worker supervisors and manag-
Insurance sales agents	Office clerks, general
Real estate brokers and sales agents	Secretaries and administrative assistants
Retail salespersons	**Farming, fishing, and forestry occupations**
Sales engineers	Agricultural workers
Sales representatives, wholesale and manufacturing	Fishers and fishing vessel operators
Sales worker supervisors	Forest, conservation, and logging workers
Securities, commodities, and financial services sales agents	**Construction trades and related workers**
Travel agents	Boilermakers
Office and administrative support occupations	Brickmasons, blockmasons, and stonemasons
Financial clerks	Carpenters
Bill and account collectors	Carpet, floor, and tile installers and finishers
Billing and posting clerks and machine operators	Cement masons, concrete finishers, & segmental pavers
Bookkeeping, accounting, and auditing clerks	Construction and building inspectors

Construction equipment operators	**Assemblers and fabricators**
Construction laborers	**Food processing occupations**
Drywall installers, ceiling tile installers, and tapers	**Metal workers and plastic workers**
Electricians	Computer control programmers and operators
Elevator installers and repairers	Machine setters, operators, and tenders—metal and plastic
Glaziers	Machinists
Hazardous materials removal workers	Tool and die makers
Insulation workers	Welding, soldering, and brazing workers
Painters and paperhangers	**Printing occupations**
Pipelayers, plumbers, pipefitters, and steamfitters	Bookbinders and bindery workers
Plasterers and stucco masons	Prepress technicians and workers
Roofers	Printing machine operators
Sheet metal workers	**Textile, apparel, and furnishings occupations**
Structural and reinforcing iron and metal workers	**Woodworkers**
Installation, maintenance, and repair occupations	**Plant and system operators**
Electrical & electronic mechanics, & repairers	Power plant operators, distributors, and dispatchers
Computer, automated teller, and office machine repairers	Stationary engineers and boiler operators
Electrical and electronics installers and repairers	Water and liquid waste treatment plant and system operators
Electronic home entertainment equipment installers and repairers	**Other production occupations**
Radio and telecommunications equipment installers and repairers	Inspectors, testers, sorters, samplers, and weighers
Vehicle & mobile equipment mechanics & repairers	Jewelers and precious stone and metal workers
Aircraft and avionics equipment mechanics and service technicians	Medical, dental, and ophthalmic laboratory technicians
Automotive body and related repairers	Painting and coating workers, except construction and mainte-
Automotive service technicians and mechanics	Photographic process workers and processing machine operators
Diesel service technicians and mechanics	Semiconductor processors
Heavy vehicle and mobile equipment service technicians & me-	**Transportation and material moving occupations**
Small engine mechanics	**Air transportation occupations**
Other installation, maintenance, & repair occupations	Air traffic controllers
Coin, vending, and amusement machine servicers and repairers	Aircraft pilots and flight engineers
Heating, air-conditioning, and refrigeration mechanics and installers	Material moving occupations
Home appliance repairers	**Motor vehicle operators**
Industrial machinery mechanics and maintenance workers	Bus drivers
Line installers and repairers	Taxi drivers and chauffeurs
Maintenance and repair workers, general	Truck drivers and driver/sales workers
Millwrights	Rail transportation occupations
Precision instrument and equipment repairers	Water transportation occupations
Production occupations	**Armed Forces occupations**

This list is reproduced with permission from Bureau of Labor Statistics, U.S. Department of Labor, *Occupational Outlook Handbook*, 2006-07 Edition (accessed January 14, 2008).

The full online edition of *OOH* can be found on our links page at www.wheresthemap.com. The *OOH* lists the degree or training requirements, working conditions, pay scale, and anticipated need for almost any career imaginable. There's also a brief overview specifically for students at this site. Print copies of the *OOH* can usually be found at a school or public library.

Any lingering thoughts or notes about how you want to make a living?

Ten Years down the Road

In ten years, I will be ___ years old. It will be the year 20___.
Here's what my life will look like:

Never let the odds
keep you from doing what you know
in your heart you were meant to do.

—H. Jackson Brown, Jr.

Chapter 5

Where in the world do you fit in?

There has never been a better time than right now for choosing where to live. The Internet allows you to explore potential homes in vivid detail without ever changing out of your pajamas. Local governments and business leaders are bending over backward to attract young, bright, talented people to their city or state. Here's what Penelope Trunk, author of *Brazen Careerist*, has to say: "Take the question of where to live seriously. Don't let inertia push you toward a big-name city, the place you grew up, or your old college haunts. Make a conscious decision to live somewhere that will improve your quality of life by really understanding what your core needs and interests are—and will be." What would your dream living situation be like? Not just the home itself, but the surroundings, the neighborhood—the works. What part of the world? Do you picture yourself putting down roots in just one place or getting around?

Do you know where you best fit in?

If **YES**, is this you?
❑ My hometown is the perfect fit for me.

You might be able to skip this chapter altogether, but then, it may help you create a mission and vision to keep you on track.

Or is this you?
❑ I have a good idea where and how I want to live, but I don't know how to make it happen.

Through the Internet, you can easily find stories from people who are living in the area you are interested in. Do some research. Talk to people about how they made their dream home possible. If money is your biggest obstacle, check out the roadblocks and detours in chapter 8 before moving on through this chapter.

Or is this you?
❑ I want to explore several places before choosing where to live.
❑ I know where I want to live, but I also want to travel to many places.

You can still start with your values, because very often these basic preferences do not change. However if you are more excited about seeing the sights, check out the travel pages in chapter 7.

Or is this you?
❑ I am very content where I am and don't have any desire to travel anywhere else.

This is perfectly fine. Maybe living somewhere else isn't your thing. Just skip that section. If you are pretty sure you'll never want to live anywhere else, you can still check out the pages where you can design your dream home.

If none of these answers seem to fit, skim through this chapter to see if it interests you. You can always come back to it later.

If **NO**, is this you?
❑ I'm not ready yet to think about where I want to live.

There's no hurry for you to think about this. But these exercises might help you figure out why— and even whether—you want to move away from home. If you have a stronger reason than "I just want to get away from my parents," you'll make your move with intention and be more content with the place you choose. Go through this chapter to identify your strongest values and preferences.

Or is this you?
❑ I don't have a clue where I want to live. Why would I need to figure this out now?

Quite honestly, you don't. However, if you have a few ideas to start with about what your values and preferences are, you will be less likely to end up in a place that isn't a great match for you. If, for example, you discover that you absolutely hate rainy weather, you could start to focus your vision on parts of the country or the world with a drier climate.

Or is this you?
❑ I want to move away, but my family would be angry/devastated/sad/hurt (pick one).

As we said earlier in chapter 3, making a choice based on your fear of disappointing someone could very well end up disappointing you down the road. Check out the roadblocks and detours in chapter 8, and also Beth's story on page 88.

Or is this you?
❑ I don't think it matters where I live. There are many more important things.

You're right, some people focus too much on the weather, or on the idea of owning a home. If you feel that there are more important things to focus on, put your attention there now. Skip this chapter and look through the other chapters to see if one speaks to you.

Values and Choices for My Place to Fit In

Maybe location is more important to you than having an elegant home. Or perhaps living near your family is key. If one of your life values is to stay out of debt, having a home may mean that you need to pay a large chunk of it up front. It could be that you don't even value a home as much as having adventure and exciting opportunities around you.

Maybe your ideal place to fit in changes constantly.

There is no one right way to choose where you live, but looking at your values will give you a good starting place. Go through the values and choices below to uncover what is most important to you about where you live. You may find some surprises!

What to do next? Go through the list of values.

 Check any that are important to you. ⭐ Star the really important ones.

❓ Question-mark any that make you go "Huh?" You can look those up later or just ignore them.

 If an important value is missing, write it in the margins.

	Location		Libraries		Community continuing education
	Rural area		Theater		**Job Market**
	Small town		Dance		Blue collar (industrial)
	Large town		Music		White collar (business)
	Suburbs		Zoos		Service industry
	Big city		Parks		Self-employment opportunities
	Big city withinan an hour of home		Sports		Work at home
	Climate		Nightlife		**Cost of living**
	Mild		Shopping		I need it to be low
	Humid		Restaurants		Right in the middle
	Dry		Good cell phone reception		High prices don't scare me!
	Sunny		High speed Internet available		**Pet Friendly**
	Lots of rain		**Physical Surroundings**		Lots of parks
	Cloudy		Desert		Animal hospitals
	Four seasons		Mountains		Pet services available
	Warm all year		Prairie		Leash laws enforced
	Colder climate		Rainforest		**Proximity to family**
	Plenty of green: trees, grass, and plants		Island		Live with my extended family
	Easy on my allergies		Seashore		Very close
	Transportation options		Woods		An hour or two away
	Airport nearby		Farmland		Have to fly to visit them
	Train station		Near water, lakes, rivers, oceans		**Diversity**
	Bus station		Natural beauty		I love ethnic diversity
	Interstate highway		**Education**		I want to be near people like me
	City bus		Good public schools		**Local Political Values**
	Train or subway		Good private schools		Conservative
	Traffic: don't want it		Home schooling support		Liberal
	Traffic: don't mind it		Community colleges		Moderate
	Culture		Private colleges/universities		Green
	Museums		Public colleges/universities		Independent

Open to alternative lifestyles	Fitness Center	Community celebrations
Crime rates	Bike trails	Town meetings
Safe secure neighborhood	**Eco-consciousness**	Everyone knows each other
Low crime a must	Recycling	Prefer to remain anonymous
Crime rates don't scare me!	Composting	**Owning or Renting**
Recreational activities	Organic foods	I must own my own home
Winter sports	Farmer's markets	Design and build my own home
Warm-weather sports	Public transportation	Renting is fine
Outdoor sports	"Green" energy sources (solar, wind)	Caretake someone else's home
Indoor sports	**Health care**	Share expenses with roommates
Hiking trails	Good doctors	House-sit from place to place
Mountains	Great hospitals	**Faith and Spirituality**
Lakes	Alternative healthcare	Beliefs similar to mine
Rivers	Special medical services available	Churches, temples, or mosques
Oceans	**Family Friendly**	Conservative religious values
Camping nearby	Good childcare options	Diverse spiritual or religious beliefs
Skate parks	Moms' groups	Liberal or progressive religious values
Parks	Children's activities and programs	Meditation groups or intention circles
Beach	**Sense of Community**	Predominantly "religious" community
Gardening	Town pride	Predominantly "secular" community

Write any starred values or choices below.

The most important values and choices for my place to fit in:

Put your values and choices in order, starting with the most important.

> #1

> #2

> #3

> #4

> #5

> #6

> #7

> #8

Find Your Spot
Do you know what you are looking for in a hometown but just don't know how to find it? Look no further than a web-based company called Find Your Spot. Find Your Spot's web site contains an interactive quiz that asks for your preferences about almost every conceivable aspect of a community, from size and climate to traffic, cultural opportunities, and cost of living, and suggests locations they think would be a great fit for you based on your answers. You can find this link at www.wheresthemap.com.

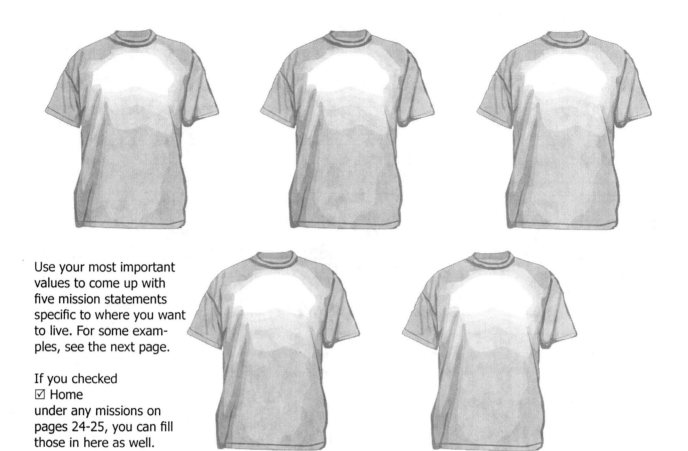

Use your most important values to come up with five mission statements specific to where you want to live. For some examples, see the next page.

If you checked
☑ Home
under any missions on pages 24-25, you can fill those in here as well.

My Primary Mission:

From your smaller mission statements, write one primary mission for a place to fit in. Remember that you can use the most important statement to represent your primary mission, or combine several.

If your mission or vision doesn't feel very strong or clear, you may just need a little more time to sort out what your focus is for where you want to live. Don't worry, there's no rush. Very often you won't know if a place fits you until you spend some time there. Usually your response will come very quickly, but sometimes a place grows on you over time.

Here are a few mission and vision statements:

Find a city that feels like home.

Stay in my hometown.

Stay in my home town

marry my high school sweetheart and build a house in my parents' neighborhood.

Find a city that feels like home

by traveling across the country in a motor home.

Establish roots and make friends in many places.

Rent a studio apartment in San Francisco.

Establish roots and make friends in many places

by teaching In American international schools around the world.

Rent a studio apartment in San Francisco

and find a social network there.

Live within an hour of my parents.

Live in a simple cabin on a lake.

Live within an hour of my parents

and raise my children close to their grandparents.

Live in a simple cabin on a lake in Wisconsin

and spend my summers fishing and water-skiing with my own motorboat.

Vision for My Place to Fit in

Now that you have written your primary mission statement, create your primary vision statement. Remember, the vision statement shows the unique way that you see yourself accomplishing your mission. The vision could expand on specifically where you want to live, what your home will feel like, or how your place to fit in combines with your work, family, or education. It should get more specific and leave you feeling more focused.

 Beth's Story

I was born in Vermont and lived in the same house until I was eighteen. My family is still there, and Vermont will always be my "home"; however, I have always felt a strong calling to see and live in other places.

In college I studied in India for four months. This idea was completely foreign to my family, who could not imagine why I would ever want to live anywhere so far away from the comforts of home. I never could describe the reason for wanting to explore this faraway land, but something within called me to try something new. After college, that same call spurred me to move west, so I packed up everything and moved to Seattle. None of my immediate family had ever made the choice to move so far away from home, but it always felt perfectly natural to me. I wanted to see how other people live, to expand my mind with how things are done in different parts of the country and the world.

Once again, a few years later, Jim and I moved to Hawaii. Why would I move even farther from home? The decision wasn't exactly based on logic. It wasn't logical to give away all our possessions and move six thousand miles from our families to an island where we knew no one, but it felt like the right decision based on the feeling in my heart. My value of exploring new places and trying new things won out over my desire to be comfortable.

Even though I really enjoy living in Hawaii, I still question whether I should move closer to my family. It is a continual process to check in with my values and my heart's response to being where I am. Over and over again, I come to the same conclusion: that this is where I best fit in—right now. This is where my overall life vision can best flourish and my life values can thrive. So despite my occasional pangs of guilt about not getting to see my family very often, I do my best to communicate with them from afar and keep working toward my life vision. I know that ultimately, as long as I am happy with my decisions, they will support me.

MY WAY / YOUR WAY

Where I best fit in:

1. Safe, secure neighborhood
2. Small, friendly community
3. Beautiful surroundings
4. High-speed Internet available
5. Area with farmer's market and organic food
6. Can work at home
7. If not near family, at least make it easy to visit them and have them visit us
8. Place to exercise, indoors or out
9. Plenty of green around: trees, grass, plants
10. Close to schools and continuing education
11. Near the ocean or mountains
12. Theater, music, and art accessible
13. Alternative health care accepted
14. Recycling and composting available
15. "Green" energy sources
16. Lots of trails for hiking

Strategies for Living, Home and My Place to Fit in

Strategies about where to live often come from family members trying to instill in you the value of home. Some come from literature, movies, or songs.

If you strongly value family, you may adopt the strategy "Home is where my family is." This strategy will keep you living near your family, which would be in line with your vision. However, if you have a travel bug and you never strongly identified with your hometown, you may seek the new experience and fresh perspective of a foreign place. You might live by the strategy "Home is wherever you are." Maybe you value your independence or freedom over almost anything else, in which case you might operate by the strategy "I cannot be free if I live near my family," and your vision would focus elsewhere, on places that enhance your sense of freedom and independence. Below are some examples of living and traveling strategies.

But the world was my home and I was glad to be in it.

—William Saroyan

Home is where you hang your hat.

Home is where your family is.

There's no place like home!

Home is wherever you are.

All journeys have secret destinations of which the traveler is unaware.

—Martin Buber

I long, as does every human being, to be at home wherever I find myself.

—Maya Angelou

One never reaches home, but wherever friendly paths intersect the whole world looks like home for a time.

—Hermann Hesse

I can find a job anywhere. It's more important to me to find a place where I fit in.

—Next Generation Consulting

Home is where the heart is.

Home is a place you grow up wanting to leave, and grow old wanting to get back to.

—John Ed

A good traveler has no fixed plans, and is not intent on arriving.

—Lao Tzu

Home is not where you live, but where they understand you.

—Christian Morganstern

Life is not measured by the number of breaths that we take, but by the places and moments that take our breath away.

—Anonymous

What are your strategies for living? Star any strategies above that are line with your values, your mission, and your vision for a place to fit in. Fill in any other useful strategies that will help support your vision.

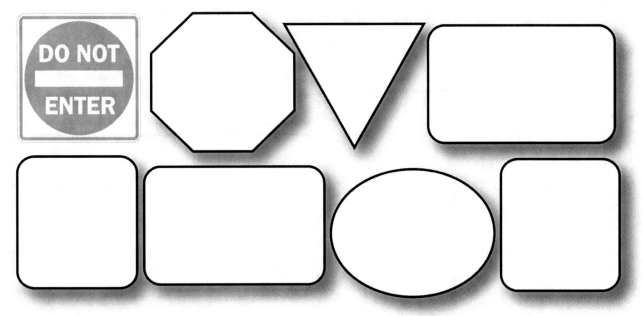

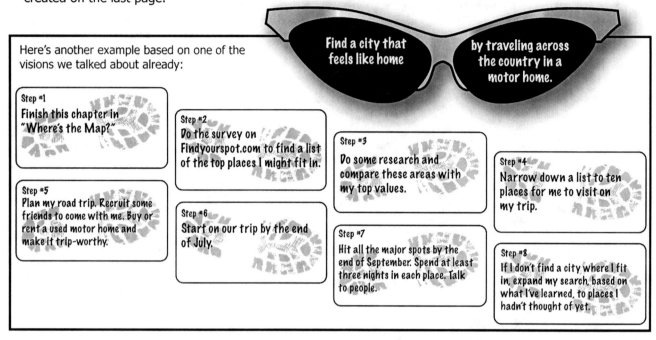

Steps for Finding My Place to Fit In

Now is a time for you to map out any steps that you think will be most important for you along the way to your vision for finding a place to fit in. Remember to base your steps on the primary vision statement you created on the last page.

Here's another example based on one of the visions we talked about already:

Find a city that feels like home *by traveling across the country in a motor home.*

Step #1
Finish this chapter in "Where's the Map?"

Step #2
Do the survey on Findyourspot.com to find a list of the top places I might fit in.

Step #3
Do some research and compare these areas with my top values.

Step #4
Narrow down a list to ten places for me to visit on my trip.

Step #5
Plan my road trip. Recruit some friends to come with me. Buy or rent a used motor home and make it trip-worthy.

Step #6
Start on our trip by the end of July.

Step #7
Hit all the major spots by the end of September. Spend at least three nights in each place. Talk to people.

Step #8
If I don't find a city where I fit in, expand my search, based on what I've learned, to places I hadn't thought of yet.

Home is the place where, when you have to go there, they have to take you in.

—Robert Frost

Step #1

Step #2

Step #3

Step #4

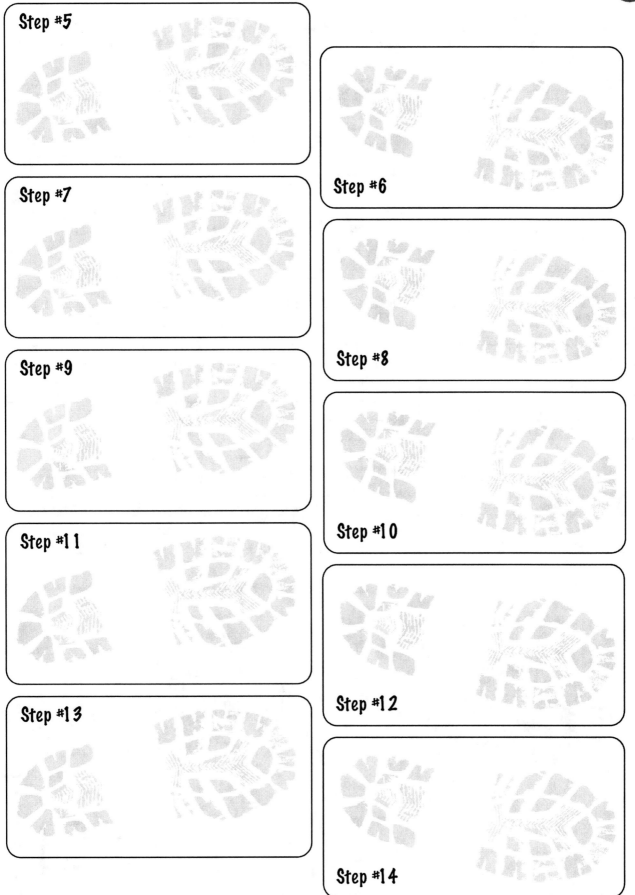

Step #5

Step #6

Step #7

Step #8

Step #9

Step #10

Step #11

Step #12

Step #13

Step #14

My Dream Home

Does your image of where you best fit in include a vision of a specific home? What does it look like? Check out the preferences below for your dream home. Later, you can put these in order of priority to keep things in perspective. For now, it's time to dream big and play around with this exercise.

	Type of Structure		Share green space with neighbors		Rooms
	Studio (one room)		Big yard with room to play		One or two bedrooms
	Apartment		Small yard, just a few trees and plants		Three to five bedrooms
	Condominium		No yard--I hate to mow		Big kitchen
	Townhouse		Flower or vegetable garden, fruit trees		Small kitchen
	Loft (converted warehouse or factory)		Pool, hot tub		Dining room
	One story house		Patio		Office
	Two or more stories		**Garage**		Mudroom
	Cabin		Big--room for many cars and storage		Home theater room
	Mansion		Normal--two cars and a lawn mower		Den/library
	Yurt/tent/teepee		Small--one car and a few boxes		Three or four season covered porch
	Trailer/RV		No garage--street parking is fine		Deck
	Location		**Floors**		Attic
	By itself in the country		Plain concrete		Basement/cellar
	Small town		Stained (colored/textured) concrete		**Environmental Options**
	City		Cork		Solar panels
	Suburbs, surrounded by similar homes		Ceramic tile		Wind power
	View		Hardwood		Solar water heater
	Nice view, mountains, lake, ocean, forest		Bamboo		Tankless instant water heater
	View doesn't matter		Regular carpet		Rainwater/gray water recycling into yard
	Size		Natural carpet (wool)		Paper, plastic, and glass recycling
	Big--privacy, lots of room to spread out		**Windows**		Yard waste composting
	Medium-- what I need but not too big		Lots of big, bright picture windows		Food waste composting
	Small and cozy		Average number and size		Natural lighting
	Yard		Windows not important		Passive solar heating and cooling

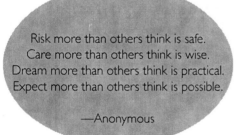

Risk more than others think is safe.
Care more than others think is wise.
Dream more than others think is practical.
Expect more than others think is possible.

—Anonymous

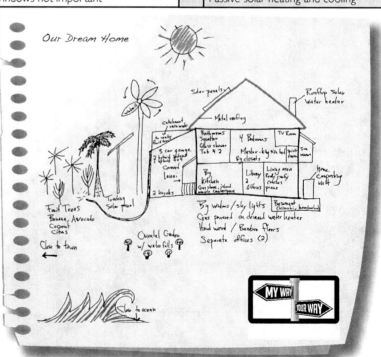

Using the checklist on the previous page along with your imagination, create the home of your dreams! If you don't have enough space, upgrade to some larger paper.

Any lingering thoughts or notes about where you fit in?

Thirty Years down the Road

In thirty years, I will be ___ years old. It will be the year 20___.
Here's what my life will look like:

> *Twenty years from now*
> *you will be more disappointed by the*
> *things you didn't do than by the ones you did.*
> *So throw off the bowlines. Sail away from the safe*
> *harbor. Catch the trade winds in your sails.*
> *Explore. Dream. Discover.*
>
> *—Unknown*

In thirty years, you will be close to the age of your parents or your friends' parents. Scary, huh? With the questions below in mind, imagine yourself as someone you know who is this age and try to come up with their answers. If you feel comfortable doing so, go ahead and interview a few of these people over the phone or in person. You might be surprised by what you hear!

❑ Are they happy with their lives?

❑ Do they have any regrets?

❑ What do they want to do with the rest of their lives?

❑ Are they happy with their jobs or careers?

❑ Do they like where they live?

❑ Is there something they have always wanted to learn but never took the time?

❑ Are they surrounded by people who support them fully?

Chapter 6

Who do you want to spend your life with?

Who would you like to accompany you on your journey through life? In the future, do you picture yourself single? In many relationships? Married? With children? How close do you want to be with your parents and relatives? Let's check in to see where you are:

Are you looking for new friends?

If **YES**, is this you?
- ❑ I like to have a large group of friends and acquaintances.
- ❑ I would like to have a best friend.
- ❑ The friends I have don't exactly know who I am or support me.
- ❑ My friends aren't the best influence on me.
- ❑ I don't have many friends right now.

You may not be able to choose your family, but you can choose your friends. Look at what qualities your current friends have. When you go through the lists, see if there are some qualities that would be a better match for who you are, who you want to be, and who you want to hang with.

If **NO**, is this you?
- ❑ I prefer having a smaller circle of friends.
- ❑ There are just a few people I feel close to, and that's fine with me!
- ❑ I have a best friend.
- ❑ I already have a boyfriend or girlfriend and don't need anyone else.
- ❑ I already have all the friends I need, and I am not looking for any more.

Okay, maybe you don't need to change your friends. If you feel basically content with the friends in your life, you may be able to skip past this chapter. Do you have any goals related to friends, family, or marriage? Before moving on, take a further peek into this chapter and see if there is something that interests you.

Or is this you?
- ❑ Friends would distract me from my goals.
- ❑ Friends are a waste of time.
- ❑ It's hard to trust anyone else.
- ❑ I'd rather be by myself.

If any of these are true for you, it could be that you haven't found the right friends. Ideally, friends should support you in your goals and make your time more enjoyable. You should be able to trust them fully. Take a look at the qualities list and see if there is anything there that you want to focus on, and then make up a vision for what your ideal friend would be.

Are you looking for a relationship?

If **YES**, is this you?
- ❑ I am not really interested in a long-term relationship, but I enjoy dating.
- ❑ I would like to have a boyfriend or girlfriend but no serious commitment.
- ❑ I'm searching for my life partner or soul mate.
- ❑ The person I'm with is not a good match for me.

The list of qualities starting on the next page gets even more specific about what you are looking for in a relationship, and even what the person might look like. If it sounds like fun to you to design this ideal mate, take a look. This doesn't mean that you will ignore anyone who doesn't fit this description. This chapter will just help you get more focused about what your priorities are.

If **NO**, is this you?
- ❑ I'm already in the perfect relationship.

Excellent! Maybe you don't need to get any further into this chapter. If it's pretty serious, you may want to take a look at your values and your partner's values and see how close they match before making any serious decisions.

Or is this you?
- ❑ I prefer being alone.
- ❑ I'm waiting for something.
- ❑ Relationships stink!
- ❑ I'm not relationship material.
- ❑ I've been hurt too many times.
- ❑ I already have lots of great friends and I would hate to mess that up.
- ❑ There are no good choices where I am.
- ❑ A relationship would distract me from my goals.
- ❑ I've screwed up relationships in the past, and I'm not looking for another one anytime soon.

If any of these are true for you, it could be that you haven't found the right person or relationship. Or maybe it's not necessary for you to be in a relationship, at least right now. To help you get clear about what you are looking for, take a look at the qualities list. See if there is anything there that you want to focus on, and then make up a vision for what your ideal relationship would be. Or perhaps another chapter is more interesting.

Are you interested in marriage?

(Not necessarily right now.)

If **YES**, is this you?

❑ I am looking for a soul mate who understands me inside and out.

❑ I am looking for someone I can share all aspects of my life with: friends, work, hobbies—everything.

❑ I am looking for someone that I am absolutely "head over heels" in love with.

❑ I want my life partner also to be my best friend.

❑ I am looking for a loving, committed relationship, but I want to keep some of my life private.

❑ I am looking for stability and comfort, but I don't necessarily need—or even believe in the idea of—a soul mate.

❑ I just want someone to keep me warm and help pay the bills.

If **NO**, is this you?

❑ I do want to share my life with someone, but I don't necessarily want to get married.

❑ I don't see any need to commit to one person—that limits me too much.

Whether marriage is in your sights or not, do you have any specific goals related to the person or people you want to spend your life with? What is most important to you about the quality of your relationships? Use whichever box you checked to help in writing your vision for marriage or relationships.

How close do you want to be to your family?

❑ I would like to live with my parents/grandparents/relatives for a few more years.

❑ I would like to live in the same town or neighborhood as my parents/grandparents/relatives.

❑ I would like for my family to be a part of my life, to see them multiple times per week.

❑ I would like for my family to be a part of my life, to see them maybe once a week or a few times per month.

❑ I don't necessarily need to live in the same town as my family, as long as I am within a few hours' drive.

❑ I don't need to live in the same part of the country as my family, as long as I can keep in contact with them by telephone and visit them once a year.

❑ I am not very close to my family, and I don't need to live near them or even be able to keep in touch.

Whatever you answer here, being clear about your priorities with your family and with where you want to live will help you design your future visions. Use these statements to help you write your vision for family.

Do you want to have children?

(Again, not necessarily right now.)

If **YES**, is this you?

❑ I would like to get married and begin having children immediately.

❑ I want children, but I would like to wait until I've been married at least a few years.

❑ I would like to adopt children.

❑ I want children, but not until I have accomplished certain goals.

❑ I want a big family with more than three kids.

❑ I don't need to be married to have children.

If **NO**, is this you?

❑ I'm not really into kids.

❑ Children would distract me from my goals.

❑ There is some other reason I **don't** want them or can't have them.

Whether children are in your future or not, these ideas will be helpful for you as you design your life vision. If you have a vision that involves having a big family, you may be less likely to match up with someone who doesn't value this.

Do you want your family to help raise your children?

If **YES**, is this you?

❑ I would like my parents or relatives to play a significant role in raising my children, perhaps as care providers while I am at work.

❑ I want my family to be a part of my children's lives; a few times per month is enough.

❑ I want my children to know my family even if I live far away from them; this would include frequent telephone contact and extended time with them during vacations.

If **NO**, is this you?

❑ I don't have very good relationships with my relatives.

❑ I have a very different lifestyle or parenting style that they do not understand, and I would therefore like to limit my children's contact with them.

Maybe these questions seem a little too far in the future for you to answer right now. But they may help you clarify your future goals for your family, marriage, and children.

> **If none of these answers seem to fit, skim through this chapter to see if it interests you. You can always come back to it later.**

Qualities for My Friendships and Relationships

What are you looking for in a friend, a group of friends, or a romantic relationship? Do you like to hang out with people who share your views, or people you can debate with? Are your friends or partners usually people who do the same things you do, enjoying the same music, sports, and hobbies, or do they have different interests?

Below is a list of qualities that you may be looking for in a friendship or a romantic relationship. The second part of the list gets much more detailed about physical

characteristics. If you are really not particular about what the person looks like, you can skip that part. But if you've always dreamed of dating a blond surfer, then this section may be essential to your vision.

You may want to go through the list first and underline the qualities that you think you have. You may also want to mark the qualities of your friends with one color and use another color for a future boyfriend, girlfriend, lover, spouse, or soul mate.

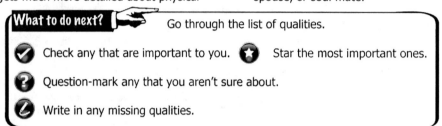

What to do next? Go through the list of qualities.

✔ Check any that are important to you.   ★ Star the most important ones.

❓ Question-mark any that you aren't sure about.

✎ Write in any missing qualities.

Accepting	Curious	Frugal	Kind
Adaptable	Decisive	Fun	Knowledgeable
Aggressive	Deep	Generous	Lazy
Altruistic	Dependable	Graceful	Lively
Ambitious	Determined	Grateful	Logical
Anal	Different interests	Happy	Loves to tell stories
Artistic	Different social background	Hardworking	Loyal
Assertive	Dignified	Healthy	Marriage
Athletic	Dutiful	Helpful	Mature
Attentive	Easygoing	Honest	Mellow
Attractive	Educated	Humorous	Meticulous
Aware	Empowering	Imaginative	Mindful
Balanced	Entertaining	Impatient	Modest
Bossy	Enthusiastic	Impulsive	Moody
Brave	Expressive	Indecisive	Motivated
Calm	Extravagant	Independent	Musical
Chaste	Extroverted	Inquisitive	Mysterious
Cheerful	Fair	Insightful	Narcissistic
Confident	Family-values oriented	Inspired	Neat
Considerate	Fashion conscious	Intelligent	Obedient
Content	Financially independent	Intimate	Open minded
Cool	Financially secure	Introverted	Optimistic
Cooperative	Firm	Joking	Organized
Creative	Flexible	Joyful	Original
Credible	Free spirited	Just	Outgoing

Outrageous	Punctual	Serene	Talented
Passionate	Realistic	Sexy	Talkative
Patriotic	Reasonable	Shrewd	Thoughtful
Peaceful	Rebellious	Silly	Thrifty
Perceptive	Refined	Similar interests	Tidy
Perfect	Relaxed	Sincere	Timid
Perky	Reliable	Skilled	Trustworthy
Philanthropic	Religious	Sociable	Understanding
Plans for the future	Reserved	Social	Unique
Playful	Responsible	Spiritual	Visionary
Popular	Sarcastic	Spontaneous	Vital
Powerful	Self-confident	Spunky	Wealthy
Practical	Selfish	Stable	Well traveled
Proactive	Selfless	Strong	Will do anything for you
Professional	Sensitive	Successful	Wise
Prosperous	Sensual	Supportive	Witty

Getting very specific...

Height	Green eyes	Hair	Race and Ethnicity
Tall	Brown eyes	Long	Same racial background
Short	Hazel eyes	Short	Different race or ethnicity
Petite	Steel gray eyes	Medium length	Born in same country
Medium height	**Skin**	Shoulder length	Born in foreign country
Body	Fair	Black	**Language**
Cute	Dark	Fair	Foreign accent
Hot	Olive	Dark	Speaks same language
Thin	Pale	Red	Share second language
Full-fugured	Tanned	Gray	**Age**
Plump	Clear/Perfect	Salt-and-pepper	Younger
Curvaceous	Freckles	Light brown	Older
Muscular	**Face**	Blond	Same age
Athletic	Baby face	White	**Sexual Orientation**
Stocky	Handsome	Curly	Gay
Well-built	Beautiful	Spiky	Straight
Skinny	Facial hair	Straight	Lesbian
Eye Color	Clean-shaven	Wavy	Bisexual
Blue eyes	Great teeth	Bald	Transgendered

The most important qualities for my friendships or relationships:

Now, put these qualities in order, starting with the most important.

Friendships

#1

#2

#3

#4

#5

#6

#7

#8

Relationships

#1

#2

#3

#4

#5

#6

#7

#8

If you are looking for a friendship or relationship, what would your classified ad say?

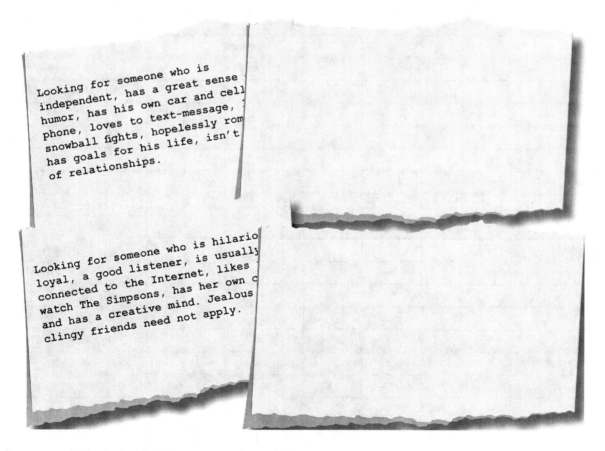

Looking for someone who is independent, has a great sense humor, has his own car and cell phone, loves to text-message, snowball fights, hopelessly rom has goals for his life, isn't of relationships.

Looking for someone who is hilario loyal, a good listener, is usually connected to the Internet, likes watch The Simpsons, has her own c and has a creative mind. Jealous clingy friends need not apply.

Use your most important values to come up with five mission statements specific to friendships, family, and relationships. For examples, see the next page.

If you checked
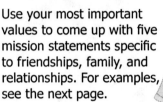 Relationships
under any missions on pages 24-25, you can fill those in here as well.

My Primary Mission:

From your smaller mission statements, write one primary mission related to the people you want to spend your life with. Remember that you can use the most important mission to represent your primary mission, or mix and match.

This mission is more a guiding principle than a hard-and-fast rule. You might say something here that in a few years is no longer true. This is totally fine. This activity should be fun for you.

Who do you want to spend your life with?

Here are a few mission and
vision statements:

Communicate
better with my
parents.

Marry
someone who is
financially
stable.

Marry someone
who is financially
stable,

who gives me
freedom to hang out
with my friends and
"do my own thing."

Communicate
better with my
parents

so they can
understand my
vision and support
me in it.

Raise a
multi-ethnic
family.

Find a group
of friends
who are more
like me.

Raise a multi-
ethnic family

by adopting
children from
several other
countries.

Find a group of
friends who are
more like me

and who let me be
myself without
hiding anything.

Meet my
soul mate.

Support my
grandmother as
she grows older.

Meet my soul
mate,

settle down on a
tropical island
and have lots of
children.

Support my
grandmother as
she grows older,

by staying near
home and manag-
ing her health
care.

Vision for My Friendships, Family, and Relationships

Now that you have written your primary mission statement, create your primary vision statement. Remember, the vision statement shows the unique way that you see yourself accomplishing your mission. The vision could expand on what you are looking for in a relationship, how you want others to see you, or where you want to live, or give a timeline for your relationships. It should leave you feeling more focused.

Beth's Story

If you had asked me after I graduated from college whether I would ever get married, I would probably have checked this box:

❏ I do want to share my life with someone, but I don't necessarily want to get married.

At the end of high school and into college I mostly hung out with friends and boyfriends who viewed marriage as "giving in to the system." As a women's rights advocate, I thought that marriage would somehow limit my freedom as a woman.

After a big break-up my senior year of college, I met Jim. He had been raised in the Catholic Church and had very different values about marriage. He valued this union of two people highly, even saw it as necessary for any relationship to become serious. Falling in love with him, I had some preconceptions that I had to get over to realize that marriage in itself was not a bad thing. Sure there are bad marriages, and plenty of women have their freedom limited after getting married. On the surface, I thought that certain qualities, especially the "coolness factor," were essential for my romantic relationships.

After meeting Jim, I discovered that certain values that I had not found in my other relationships were essential to a marriage. Commitment, comfort, and having my husband be my best friend took top priority in my values for marriage. Something must be working, because we have been married seven years now and haven't gotten sick of each other yet!

New Ways of Meeting People

Just a few years ago, people were pretty much limited to meeting others in their local area. If you were looking for a new drummer for your band, you would put up a flyer at the local music store. If you wanted a group to play basketball with, you looked for them at the gym or the Y. Finding someone to date usually happened at school, a party, a club or organization you both belonged to, or through a friend. While these methods still work, the Internet has introduced a whole new dynamic to finding and meeting people.

Now if you are looking for a new drummer for your band, you can search for one using sites such as Ask.com, Facebook, and Craig's List. You are just a Google click away from an ultimate-Frisbee group that meets near you. Looking for friendship or love? Try MySpace, Match.com, or the Yahoo Personals. Besides being easy to use and, for the most part, free, these sites are great because they take much of the discomfort out of meeting new people.

Have you ever been anxious about saying hello to that girl you see at the park occasionally, or walking up to a group of people at a party or event, fearing that sting of rejection? Meeting people online is easy. Looking for people who like to talk about or play your favorite sport? If so, join their group, check them out, and, if you like what you see, stay with them. If they're local, go hang out with them. If, after checking out their posts, you find them a little weird, no problem—look elsewhere. The same goes for friendships or relationships. Check out the profiles of people you might be interested in. If you like what you see, send them a message to check out your profile. Simple and relatively painless. Don't forget to be safe: there are also web sites that allow you to do background checks.

Who do you want to spend your life with?

Strategies for My Friendships, Family, and Relationships

Is your family more important than friends? If so, you may guide your life by the strategy "Family comes first." Or maybe you have a family member who had a bad experience being married, and this shaped your perception. Your strategy may have become "I will never be happy in a marriage".

Do the strategies that you live your life by serve you, your friendships, and your relationships? Take a look at the quotes below and see if any of them make sense to you. Star any that you especially like.

The best relationships--friendship and otherwise--tend to be those where you can say anything to the other person but you don't say everything.

—Audrey Beth Stein

Love in marriage should be the accomplishment of a beautiful dream, and not, as it too often is, the end.

—Alphonse Karr

It seems essential, in relationships and all tasks, that we concentrate only on what is most significant and important.

—Søren Kierkegaard

The love of a family is life's greatest blessing.

—Anonymous

Be who you are and say what you feel because those who mind don't matter and those who matter don't mind.

—Dr. Seuss

When we are in love we seem to ourselves quite different from what we were before.

—Anonymous

Happiness is having a large, loving, caring, close-knit family in another city.

—George Burns

It's the friends you can call up at 4 a.m. that matter.

—Marlene Dietrich

Other things may change us, but we start and end with family.

—Anthony Brandt

Love is liking someone better than you like yourself.

—Anonymous

Call it a clan, call it a network, call it a tribe, call it a family: Whatever you call it, whoever you are, you need one.

—Jane Howard

I love people. I love my family, my children ...but inside myself is a place where I live all alone and that's where you renew your springs that never dry up.

—Pearl S. Buck

It is one of the blessings of old friends that you can afford to be stupid with them.

—Ralph Waldo Emerson

Making the decision to have a child - it's momentous. It is to decide forever to have your heart go walking outside your body.

—Elizabeth Stone

Your friends are God's way of apologizing for your relatives.

—Dr. Wayne Dyer

Friendship is born at that moment when one person says to another: 'What! You, too? I Thought I was the only one.'

—C.S. Lewis

Quotes often make easy strategies because you don't have to come up with them on your own. You can always find great quotes on the web, so if nothing works for you here, look up "family", "relationships", "friends," or "children" on any of the quote web sites online. Go ahead and fill in any strategies that work for you below.

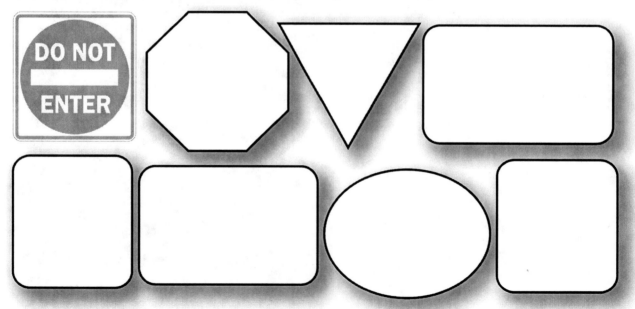

Steps for My Friendships, Family, and Relationships

Now it's time for you to map out the most important steps for you to realize your vision for the people you want to spend your life with. Remember to base your steps on the primary vision statement you already created. Steps don't always have to be done in a particular order; they can simply be a list of goals that lead you toward your vision.

Here's another example based on one of the visions we talked about already:

Raise a multi-ethnic family by adopting children from several other countries.

Step #1
Find the perfect partner who also dreams of having a multi-ethnic family.

Step #2
Research options for adoption and understand how it works.

Step #3
Research the areas of the world where adoption is accepted and much needed.

Step #4
Research the best adoption agencies to work with.

Step #5
Apply for an international adoption with our chosen agency.

Step #6
Save up enough money to process the paperwork for adoption and transportation costs.

Step #7
If the adopted child is of speaking age, take classes in the child's language. Become bilingual in that language.

Step #8
Provide a warm and welcoming home for our emerging family. Share information with our child about her or his culture.

Live with intention.
Walk to the edge. Listen hard.
Practice wellness. Play with abandon. Laugh.
Choose with no regret. Continue to learn.
Appreciate your friends. Do what you love.
Love as if this is all there is.

—Mary Anne Radmacher

Step #1

Step #2

Step #3

Step #4

Who do you want to spend your life with?

Step #5

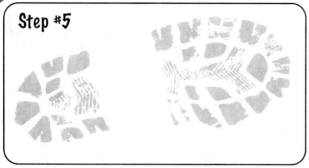

Step #6

Step #7

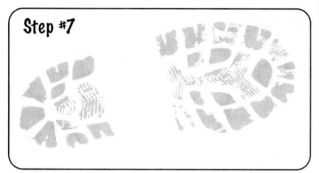

Step #8

Step #9

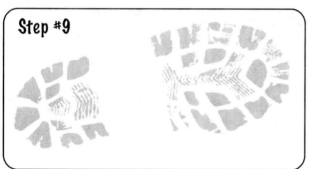

Step #10

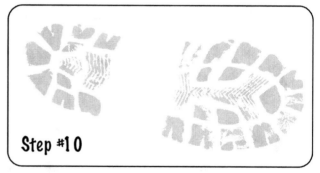

Step #11

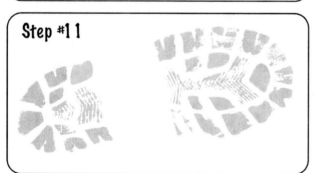

Step #12

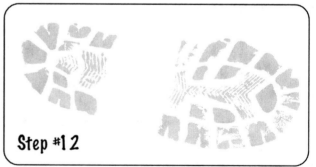

Step #13

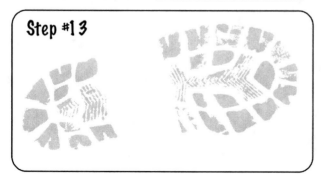

Step #14

Any lingering thoughts or notes about who you want to spend your life with?

Who do you want to spend your life with?   111

Fifty Years down the Road

In fifty years, I will be ___ years old. It will be the year 20___.
Here's what my life will look like:

How old would you be if you didn't know how old you are?

—Unknown

In fifty years you will be around the age of your grandparents or your friends' grandparents today. What do they value about their lives? What do they regret? What do they see as their biggest successes?

If your grandparents are alive, give them a call or a visit and ask them a few questions about their lives. You could also stop in at a retirement home to volunteer for an afternoon. You will not only make their day; you may also learn something new about who they are and who they wish they had been.

Using what they tell you, how do you want to see the world and your life when you are their age?

Chapter 7

What keeps you going?

Is there something that recharges your batteries when you're tired or stressed out? If you have a vision, this may be enough to keep you excited about life and eager to wake up the next morning. But even with a vision, you may find that you need other ways to relax, recharge, and enjoy your time. For you, maybe this is traveling, listening to opera, playing tennis, or meditating. This is the place to check in when you feel overwhelmed and need to get centered, chill out, or relax. It's also the place to come when you are looking for a little more inspiration.

Do you know what keeps you going?

If **YES**, is this you?
❏ The people in my life really keep me going.

Chapter 6 may be the most interesting to you. If you have certain things such as traveling, spirituality, or hobbies that you enjoy doing with others, you may want to take a look at this chapter.

Or is this you?
❏ I have a hobby that I turn to when I'm feeling burned out or frustrated by life.

Do you have any goals related to your hobby? Maybe you have always wanted to compete nationally or receive an award for your talent. If you're interested in setting some goals, keep reading this chapter. If you prefer to do your hobby free from any pressures or future expectations, you may be able to skip this chapter altogether.

Or is this you?
❏ My spiritual life, beliefs, or religion fuels me the most.

There are a few pages at the end of this chapter that go into greater depth about your spiritual beliefs. That's the place to set any goals or visions related to your spiritual life. Maybe you have always wanted to make a pilgrimage to some sacred sites in Europe or take a Native American vision quest.

Or is this you?
❏ My life vision keeps me going. It's all I need.

Wonderful! This is the ideal scenario, in which your vision keeps you excited enough about life that you can work toward it without ever getting that all-too-common feeling of being burned out. If this ever changes, remember first that your vision may have evolved and also that you may just need a little break before getting back to work on your vision. In the meantime, you can find some things to do that make you feel connected again.

Or is this you?
❏ Traveling is what keeps me going.

At the end of this chapter are some pages dedicated to travel, and you may also want to check out chapter 4 to see if a gap year can satisfy your travel bug.

If **NO**, is this you?
❏ I just live day to day. Not much thrills me. I'm pretty bored with life.

Are you content with this? If you are looking for something more out of life, maybe you haven't figured out your life vision or identified any strong purpose for living. Flip back to chapter 1 and check out Wheresthe-map.com for sample visions to see if anything inspires you.

Or is this you?
❏ I don't know what keeps me going. There are a few things I like to do, but nothing's especially exciting.

Go through this chapter to see if anything sparks your attention. Maybe there's something you have always wanted to try but never had the time for. Also, be sure to go through chapter 1 to create your life vision, since this may be where you find what keeps you going.

Or is this you?
❏ I don't see the point in even asking this question.

You may want to skip this chapter if it doesn't have any meaning for you. What keeps you going is about anything that makes your life worth living from day to day. If you haven't found a vision, maybe there's something else that keeps you excited to wake up in the morning. This chapter will help you sort out what that may be.

> **If none of these answers seem to fit, skim through this chapter to see if it interests you. You can always come back to it later.**

Choices for What Keeps Me Going

Does reading a great book keep you up till the middle of the night, or would you prefer to spend every waking moment backpacking? The list below represents some of the many ways that you can relax, play, recharge, and simply enjoy life even more.

Is there anything on the list that you are already excited about? Anything that you really want to learn in the future? Do you participate for fun, or do you have a goal to achieve something within a particular sport, hobby, or activity?

What to do next? Go through the list of hobbies and pastimes.

- ✓ Check any that are important to you.
- ★ Star the most important ones.
- ❓ Question-mark any that make you pause, in case you want to look them up later.
- ✎ Write in any missing pastimes.

	Aerobics		Chemical experiments		GPS drawing
	Airsoft		Coin collecting		Graphic design
	Animal rescue		Computer games		Hacky sack
	Animation design		Computer programming		Hiking
	Antique cars		Cooking		Historical reenactment
	Antique collecting		Cricket		Historical trekking
	Archery		Crochet		Home repairs
	Arts and crafts		Cycling		Horoscopes
	Astrology		Dance		Horseback riding
	Astronomy		Dog breeding		Hunting
	Auto customizing		Drawing		Ice skating
	Autocross		Electronics		Image editing
	Backpacking		E-mailing		Interactive fiction
	Badminton		Erector Sets		Interactive storytelling
	Baseball, softball		Falconry		Interior design
	Basketball		Fantasy sports		Jewelry making
	Beekeeping		Fencing		Juggling
	Bird-watching		Film-making		Kit cars
	Bird feeding		Fireworks		Kite flying
	Blacksmithing		Fishing		Kite surfing
	Blogging		Fishkeeping		Knitting
	Board games		Flying		Lacrosse
	Bookcrossing		Football		Laser skirmish
	Bouldering		Foreign languages		Literature
	Bowling		Gardening		Locksmithing
	Butterfly watching		Geocaching		Magic tricks
	Calligraphy		Geyser gazing		Martial arts
	Camping		Ghost hunting		Meditation
	Canoeing and kayaking		Glassblowing		Model building
	Card games		Gliding		Motorcycles
	Caving		Golf		Mountain climbing
	Cheerleading		Gossiping		Movies, TV

Music		Robots		Surfing
Musical composition		Rock climbing		Survival camping
MySpace		Rockhounding		Swimming
Newsgroups		Role-playing games		Table tennis
Observation		Rowing		Tennis
Off-roading		Running, jogging		Toys
Online virtual realities		Sailing		Transportation
Outdoor/nature activities		Scrapbooking		Traveling
Paintball		Scuba diving		Treasure hunting
Painting		Sculpture		Trucks
Partying		Sewing		Ultimate Frisbee
People/crowd watching		Shopping		Urban exploration
Performing arts		Shooting guns		Video games
Pets		Sightseeing		Volleyball
Photography		Singing		Walking
Physics experiments		Skating		Wargaming
Playing musical instruments		Skiing		Watching television
Pottery		Snorkeling		Weaving
Quilting		Snowboarding		Web surfing
Racquetball		Soapmaking		Weightlifting
Radio controllled toys		Soccer		Wikipedia
Rafting		Songwriting		Wood carving
Rallying		Spirituality and Religion		Woodworking
Reading		Stamp collecting		Writing
Retrocomputing		Stone skipping		Yachting
Ringette		Sunbathing		Yoga

Write out any starred interests below.

My favorite ways to relax, chill, have fun, or enjoy life:

Now, put your interests in order, starting with the most important.

#1

#2

#3

#4

#5

#6

#7

#8

What keeps you going?   115

It may seem strange to have a mission statement for how you keep yourself going. Sometimes, though, you might be in the middle of a stressful time and need a little reminder of your other missions to keep things in perspective or just to play for a little while before getting back to the task at hand.

You don't need to come up with missions for having fun if that takes the fun out of it. This section is more for you if you have a particular goal or accomplishment associated with an activity. Take a look at the missions on the previous page to get an idea of how you might take the key activities you enjoy and give them some goals.

If you checked
☑ Hobbies/pastimes
under any missions on pages 24-25, you can fill those in here as well.

My Primary Mission:

From your smaller mission statements, write one primary mission for what keeps you going.

Here are a few mission and vision statements:

Learn to play the guitar.

Train for the Honolulu Marathon.

Train for the Honolulu Marathon

and complete it in under four hours.

Learn to play the guitar

and be part of a small rock band.

Spread my faith and help others in need.

Learn to scuba dive.

Spread my faith and help others in need

by attending a mission trip to Mexico with my church.

Learn to scuba dive

and dive in five of the top ten diving sites around the world.

Take life less seriously.

Visit all fifty states.

Take life less seriously

by having fun in everything I do.

Visit all fifty states

collect a postcard from each one, and assemble a scrapbook.

Vision for What Keeps Me Going

Now that you have written your primary mission statement, create your primary vision statement. Remember, the vision statement shows the unique way that you see yourself accomplishing your mission. The vision could expand on a special award or achievement, a specific place or ceremony, who you want to incorporate into your mission, or how it will be accomplished. It should get more specific and leave you feeling more focused.

What Keeps Me Going: Surfing

For me, surfing is a way to connect with my sense of inner calm at the same time that I'm completely immersed in thrilling, dynamic motion. Surfing brings out my passion and my sense of fulfillment, recharging my batteries whenever life runs them down. When I'm surfing, I am wholly present in what I'm doing. It isn't a planned or calculated thing—in fact, it's about the most fluid and spontaneous expression I can think of. It's when I feel the closest to God, to the creator and mover of everything. When I paddle out past the breakers, I am transported to another place, having left all the baggage of daily life back on the beach—there's just no room for thoughts about work, relationships, or life's big and little problems.

I see the ocean and the waves as a force of nature that's always changing, and I'm in there, too, ready to ride that flow and roll with the changes. When I'm paddling my board out, there is nobody else out there to tell me what to do, cheer me on, or bring me safely back into shore—it's just me and that long, gorgeous set of waves. Each wave requires impeccable intuition and decisive action. Do I drop in on this one or wait for the next? I must be fully present to decide, especially on those bigger waves. The bigger the wave, the more crucial my skills, my confidence, my ability to commit fully. Even the slightest hesitation can affect my performance, with potentially scary consequences.

Why do I do it? It's a package, really—a big, multifaceted package. I do it for the love of the movement, the thrill, the connecting with God within myself and with nature and the ocean; for the adrenaline and the opportunity to be fully present, to be NOW, and to express myself creatively on the waves. I don't try to bend my head around calculated strategies, because it doesn't work—I just deal with changes in the wave as they come, and in the process, there's this beautiful dance that occurs between me and that irresistible force we call the ocean.

Surfing's my passion. What's yours? There's no sin in not knowing, as long as you're searching. Always follow your bliss.

Aloha,
Matt Terrusa
Licensed Acupuncturist

Strategies for What Keeps Me Going

Did you grow up believing that you had to be productive every moment of the day and did not have permission to relax? This may have formed a strategy such as "The work is never done," which you now use to guide your free time.

On the other hand, if you learned to rebel against the rules of society in order to enjoy your life more fully, maybe the strategy "If you obey all the rules, you miss all the fun" is more appropriate for you.

What strategies make the most sense to you? The statements and quotes below are predominantly related your hobbies, having fun, and spending your free time. If you value money most or have a strong connection to your faith, your strategies for what keeps you going will reflect those values.

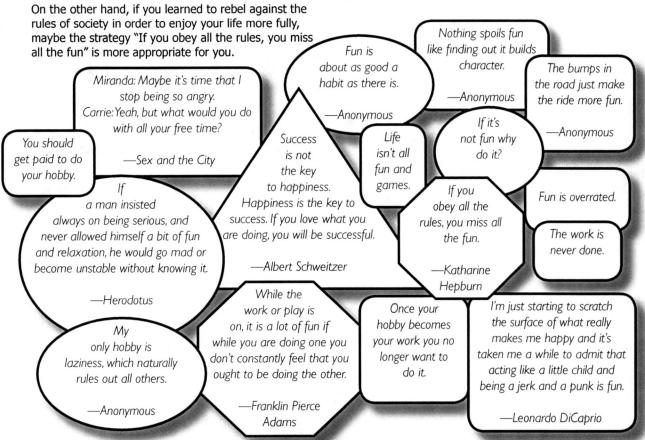

Miranda: Maybe it's time that I stop being so angry. Carrie: Yeah, but what would you do with all your free time?
—Sex and the City

You should get paid to do your hobby.

Fun is about as good a habit as there is.
—Anonymous

Nothing spoils fun like finding out it builds character.
—Anonymous

The bumps in the road just make the ride more fun.
—Anonymous

Success is not the key to happiness. Happiness is the key to success. If you love what you are doing, you will be successful.
—Albert Schweitzer

Life isn't all fun and games.

If it's not fun why do it?

Fun is overrated.

If a man insisted always on being serious, and never allowed himself a bit of fun and relaxation, he would go mad or become unstable without knowing it.
—Herodotus

If you obey all the rules, you miss all the fun.
—Katharine Hepburn

The work is never done.

My only hobby is laziness, which naturally rules out all others.
—Anonymous

While the work or play is on, it is a lot of fun if while you are doing one you don't constantly feel that you ought to be doing the other.
—Franklin Pierce Adams

Once your hobby becomes your work you no longer want to do it.

I'm just starting to scratch the surface of what really makes me happy and it's taken me a while to admit that acting like a little child and being a jerk and a punk is fun.
—Leonardo DiCaprio

What are your strategies for what keeps you going? Star any strategies above that are line with your values, your mission, and your vision for a place to fit in. Fill in any other useful strategies that will help support your vision.

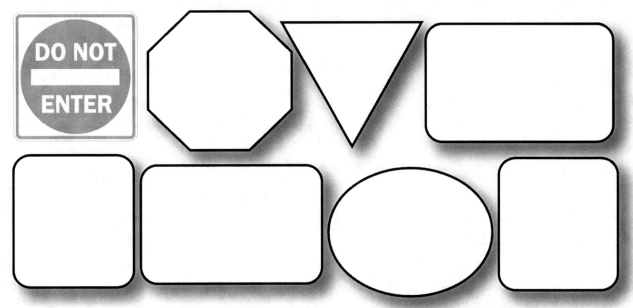

Steps for What Keeps Me Going

Now is the time for you to map out the most important steps to help you realize your primary vision.

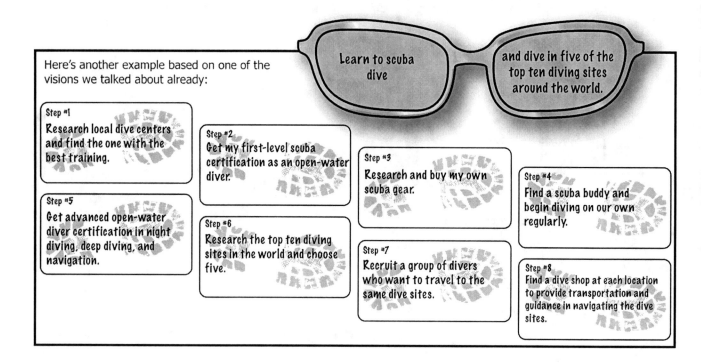

Here's another example based on one of the visions we talked about already:

Learn to scuba dive and dive in five of the top ten diving sites around the world.

Step #1
Research local dive centers and find the one with the best training.

Step #2
Get my first-level scuba certification as an open-water diver.

Step #3
Research and buy my own scuba gear.

Step #4
Find a scuba buddy and begin diving on our own regularly.

Step #5
Get advanced open-water diver certification in night diving, deep diving, and navigation.

Step #6
Research the top ten diving sites in the world and choose five.

Step #7
Recruit a group of divers who want to travel to the same dive sites.

Step #8
Find a dive shop at each location to provide transportation and guidance in navigating the dive sites.

It's not the years in your life that count.
It's the life in your years.

—Abraham Lincoln

Step #1

Step #2

Step #3

Step #4

Step #5

Step #6

Step #7

Step #8

Step #9

Step #10

Step #11

Step #12

Step #13

Step #14

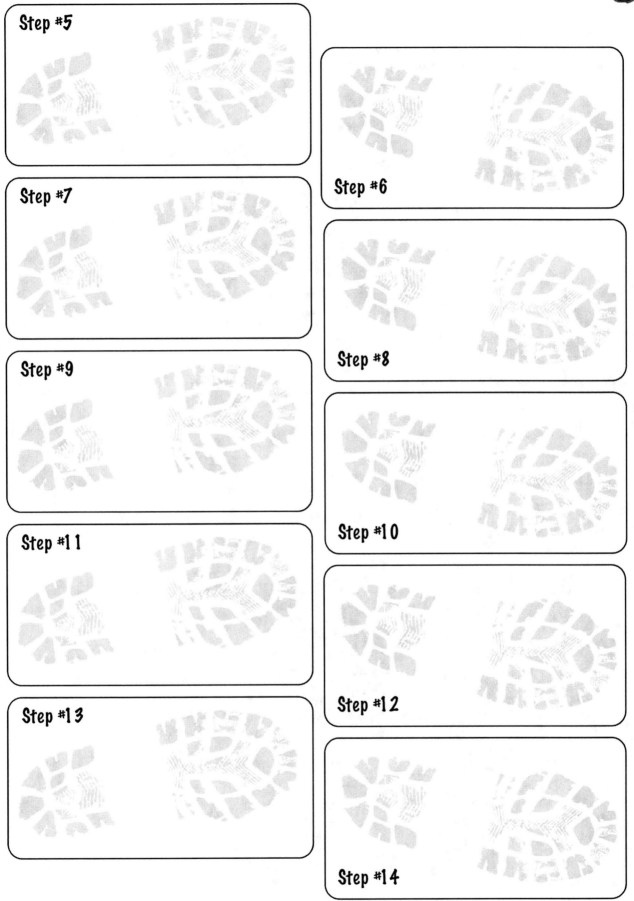

So Many Places, So Little Time...

Do you like to travel away from home, see new places, and meet new people? If you are interested in world travel or even extensive travel within your own country, here's a place to fill in some of your goals.

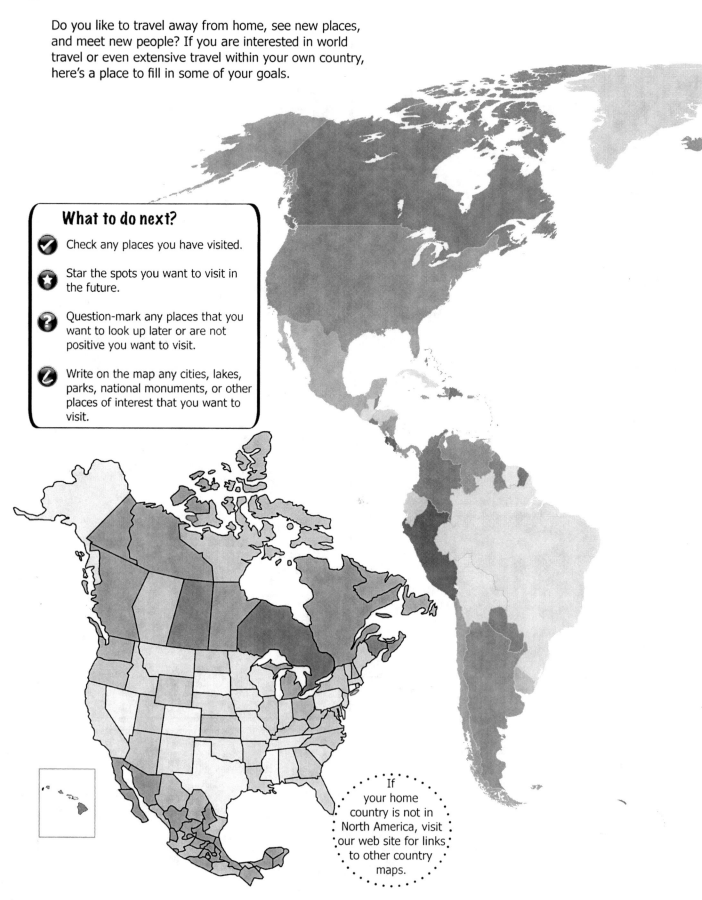

What to do next?

✔ Check any places you have visited.

★ Star the spots you want to visit in the future.

? Question-mark any places that you want to look up later or are not positive you want to visit.

✎ Write on the map any cities, lakes, parks, national monuments, or other places of interest that you want to visit.

If your home country is not in North America, visit our web site for links to other country maps.

If you don't have room, consider buying a large map and hanging it on your bedroom wall to mark all the places you would like to go. There are also some great interactive maps on the Internet to show where you have been and where you would like to visit. Visit www.wheresthemap.com for links.

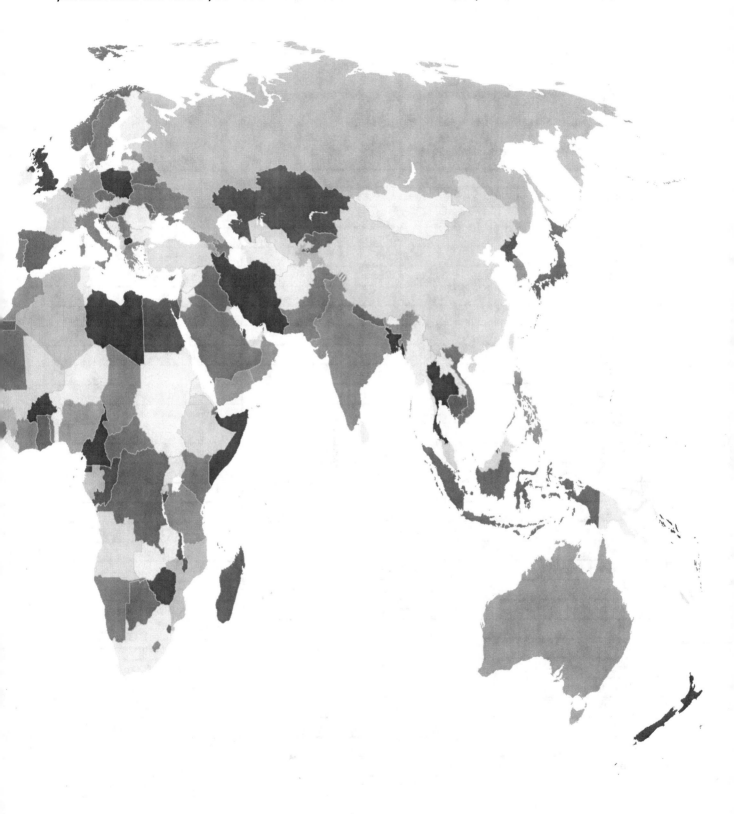

Travel Values and Choices

If travel is part of your vision for what keeps you going, this section is for you. If you are interested in travel as a hobby or simply as a way to escape for two weeks out of the year, you can start with the values and choices listed below. Narrow down the list by checking the things that most appeal to you most.

What to do next? 👉 Go through the list of values.

✔ Check any that are important to you.   ★ Star the really important ones.

❓ Question-mark any that make you go "Huh?" You can look those up later or just ignore them.

✎ If an important value is missing, write it in the margins.

Where?	Extended trips	Big cities: New York, Paris, Tokyo
Somewhere in my country	A week or two	Small cities: Venice, Anchorage, Oaxaca
In my state or region	A month or more	Quaint farming towns
Africa	A year or more	National parks
Antarctica	**How Often?**	Historic sites
Asia	Once a year	Modern marvels: Las Vegas, Dubai
Australia	Twice a year	Churches, mosques, temples
Europe	One major trip every five years	Natural wonders
North America	Many times per year	Archeological sites
South America	**Transportation?**	Castles
Pacific Islands	Car	Old West towns
National parks	Plane	Museums, music, art
Boat or ship on a river/lake/ocean	Train	Parties and nightlife
City	Boat	Light activity—hiking, biking
Small town or village	Motorcycle	Extreme sports—mountain climbing
Rural area	Bicycle	Tourist attractions
Developed world	Horse	Lying on the beach
Developing world	Camel	Cruise
World tour	Foot	**Language**
Where to Stay?	**With Whom?**	English speaking
Indoor lodging	Tour group	Second language that I know
Outdoor lodging	Friends	Completely new language
Resort and spa	Family	Very few English-speakers
Hotel	Alone	Language immersion program
Youth hostel	Friends met along the way	**Educational Opportunities**
Under the stars	**Finances**	Study abroad experience
With friends	Big budget	Research other cultures
House swap	Shoestring	College credit received
Host family	Paid work holiday	Learning on my own
How Long?	Paid opportunity	Volunteer opportunities
Short trips	**Where? What?**	Mission/religious opportunities

My favorite ways to travel:

What are your top travel values and choices? Write your most important values and any travel goals from the previous pages in the space above, and put them in order below. Then come up with a travel vision below.

#1

#2

#3

#4

#5

#6

#7

#8

Consult the lists!

You will find all kinds of lists on the Internet of amazing places to travel. Below are a few lists representing many wonders of the world, both natural and man-made. For more ideas, check out *1,000 Places to See Before You Die* by Patricia Schultz, or visit the links at www.wheres-themap.com for travel and other inspirational sites.

Underwater wonders
Great Barrier Reef
Palau
Belize Barrier Reef
Deep-sea Vents
Galápagos Islands
Lake Baikal
Northern Red Sea

Natural travel wonders
Grand Canyon
Serengeti migration
Galápagos Islands
Grand Canyon
Iguazú Falls
Amazon rain forest
Ngorongoro Crater
Victoria Falls
Bora Bora
Cappadocia

American Society of Civil Engineers Seven Wonders of the Modern World
Chunnel
CN Tower
Empire State Building
Golden Gate Bridge
Itaipu Dam
Delta Works
Panama Canal

Man-Made Wonders of Old
Giza pyramid complex
Great Wall of China
Taj Mahal
Machu Picchu
Colosseum
Stonehenge
Porcelain tower of nanjing
Leaning Tower of Pisa
Hagia Sophia
Bali
Angkor Wat
Forbidden City (China)
Catacombs of Kom el Shoqafa
Karnak temple
Teotihuacán

A Higher Purpose

Do you have a spiritual belief, faith, or religious practice that keeps you going? If you would like to explore this a little more, stay here and check out these pages. If not, go ahead and skip to the end of the chapter.

What do you believe in?

- ❑ I believe in God or a Higher Power.
- ❑ I believe that there is one true faith, the one I practice.
- ❑ I have really strong faith.
- ❑ I belong to a particular church that practices this religion: _____
- ❑ I was born into this church and will always be a part of it.
- ❑ My faith is wavering.
- ❑ It doesn't matter to me if others believe as I do.
- ❑ My beliefs are different from my parents'.
- ❑ I have changed spiritual beliefs many times in my life.
- ❑ I don't need to go to a church to have strong faith.
- ❑ I haven't found anywhere that practices what I believe.
- ❑ I don't believe there is only one true faith.
- ❑ I believe in multiple faiths and take a little truth from each of them.
- ❑ I am not religious but consider myself a very spiritual person.
- ❑ I'm still looking for something that I believe in.
- ❑ I'm pretty confused about spirituality right now.
- ❑ I don't really have time to think about my beliefs.
- ❑ I don't believe in anything.
- ❑ I don't think about this stuff at all!

How much does religion affect your personal life?

- ❑ Most of the people in my life share my faith.
- ❑ My faith is definitely something that helps keep me going.
- ❑ It is important that I marry someone who shares my beliefs.
- ❑ It is important that I share my faith with others.
- ❑ Prayer is a regular part of my life.
- ❑ Service and social justice are a part of my life every day.
- ❑ I participate in service mission trips at least once a year.
- ❑ I am very open about talking about my faith with others.
- ❑ I think it's important to attend a religious school.
- ❑ I would choose the place that I live based on my religion and the faith practiced in the area.
- ❑ I use meditation and yoga to express my spirituality.

This is what I believe:

How does your spiritual life keep you going?

- ❑ It gives me hope.
- ❑ It gives me a sense of purpose.
- ❑ It keeps me connected to something bigger than myself.
- ❑ It keeps me connected to my family.
- ❑ My group of friends practice the same faith.
- ❑ It keeps me out of trouble.
- ❑ It gives me something to do.
- ❑ _____

This discussion is brief, even though your spiritual life may play a very big role in your life decisions. Looking back at your ranked values lists at the beginning of each chapter, what values are based on your spiritual or religious beliefs? Write these values down:

Perhaps your faith is such a strong value that it is woven into all your missions for the other areas of your life. What role does your faith or spirituality play in your overall life vision? If you haven't incorporated your faith into your vision statements, go back through the chapters and see if there is a way to adapt your statements to reflect your beliefs.

#1
#2
#3
#4

Maybe you are content with your previous vision statements (or don't want to mess with them now) but would like a special place to write out a specific vision for your faith or spiritual life.
Here's a space to write that vision:

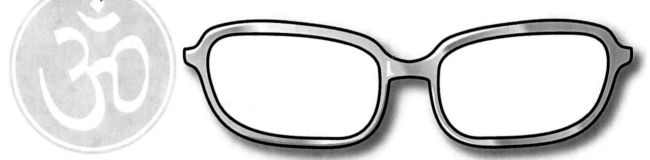

Are there any strategies based on your faith that you use to guide your life? Remember, these strategies are the road signs that keep you on track. They will often be statements that are repeated within your religious texts or by your spiritual leaders. The admonition to "turn the other cheek" is a strategy based on spiritual teachings.

Any lingering thoughts or notes about what keeps you going?

At the End of the Road

At the end of my life, as I look back on all my years,
here's what I want to find:

At the end of your life, as you look back on all the years you have lived, how do you want to feel? What was your purpose for living? What have you accomplished? How do you want to be remembered?

Beth's End of the Road:
At the end of my life, I want to look back on a life of joy. I want to remember having loads of fun with family and friends. I want to remember a lot of laughter. I want to have visited new places, stretched my limits, and taken some risks, whatever their outcomes. I want to know that I gave it my all and didn't give up.

I want to feel that I fulfilled my spiritual purpose on this Earth and that I helped a lot of people enjoy their lives a little more. I want to have published several books that are still helping others. I want to be remembered as a teacher. I would like to have provided for a family and to be really proud of my children's accomplishments. I would like to have lived in beautiful places. I want to have a lot of peace in my heart. I would like to have spent a lot of time enjoying the fresh air outdoors.

I want to have spent my life supporting the people, organizations, and causes I believe in. I want to have learned to play the piano pretty well and to have always been open to learning new things.

Part 3

Roadblocks
and
Detours

Chapter 8

What's stopping you from living the life of your dreams?

Is there something or someone stopping you from living the life you want? A **Roadblock** is something that appears to stop you, stall you, or seriously slow down your movement in the direction of your dreams. A **Detour** is simply a way to get around a roadblock, to continue in the direction you want to go. Sometimes detours seem too costly in the time or work involved, but they usually present a new solution you hadn't thought of. This chapter presents six major roadblocks and some detours to help you get around each one.

Is there something stopping you from living your life your way?

Roadblock #1: "But what would others think?"

❑ I often make decisions based on what I think my parents or friends would approve of.

❑ I don't express myself fully, because I'm afraid of what others might think.

❑ I'll do anything to uphold my reputation.

❑ I generally don't tell many people about what I'm thinking or doing, because I think they would judge me.

❑ I'd rather please other people than do what's best for me.

❑ I'm afraid I'll disappoint someone if I tell them what I really want to do with my life.

Roadblock #2: "I can't figure out what 'my way' is."

❑ I feel lost.

❑ I'm not sure what I really believe in.

❑ My parents have been telling me what to do for so long that I'm not sure what I really want to do.

❑ I don't know how to figure out what I really want to do.

❑ Sometimes I do things that don't represent "me."

❑ There are so many choices—how do I know which is the right one for me?

Roadblock #3: "But what if I fail?"

❑ I'm afraid of failing, so I'm not sure I want to try.

❑ To avoid failure, I'm planning to follow a safe and predictable career path.

❑ I'm afraid that someone I care about will say "I told you so" if I fail.

❑ What I really want to do is too risky.

❑ I don't want to be seen as a failure.

❑ I don't want to study a certain subject, because I might not be smart enough to succeed.

Roadblock #4: "But what would happen if . . ."

❑ I have a big dream, but I'm afraid to pursue it, because there are so many unknowns.

❑ I would like to do some world travel, but I'm afraid of what might happen on the road.

❑ There's a career I'm thinking about, but my parents are worried about whether I would make enough money to keep afloat.

❑ I'm thinking about moving away from home, but I'm afraid of what would happen, whether I would like it, whether I would run out of money, or something worse.

❑ There's a subject I'm interested in studying, but I don't know how I would make a living with it.

Roadblock #5: "I don't know how to make it happen."

❑ I feel stuck.

❑ I just don't think I have any options.

❑ I'll never have enough money to do what I really want to do.

❑ I'm just not feeling very creative.

❑ I can't think "outside the box."

❑ I can't come up with any solutions different from those I've already tried.

Roadblock #6: "My thoughts are controlling me!"

❑ I feel as though I'm having a continuous argument in my head.

❑ I can't make up my mind about anything.

❑ I seem to doubt my abilities more than I believe in myself.

❑ I let little things people say get to me, and I replay them in my head.

❑ One voice tells me to go for my dreams, but the other tells me I can't do it.

❑ I make up stories about things not turning out right.

❑ I can't picture a happy ending to my life.

❑ I'm not good enough, smart enough, or talented enough to pursue the life I really want.

Where to go from here?

Did you relate to any of the roadblocks above? If you could use a few ideas on how to detour around these roadblocks, this chapter is worth spending some time on.

If none of these roadblocks is an issue for you right now, you can always come back to this chapter later should a roadblock come up while you're working through the book—or at any point down the road when something blocks your way.

ROAD BLOCK

#1: "But what would others think?"

I cannot give you the formula for success, but I can give you the formula for failure, which is: Try to please everybody.

—Herbert Swope

Do any of these describe you?

❑ I often make decisions based on what I think my parents or friends would approve of.

❑ I don't express myself fully because I'm afraid of what others might think.

❑ I'll do anything to uphold my reputation.

❑ I generally don't tell many people about what I'm thinking or doing, because I think they would judge me.

❑ I'd rather please other people than do what's best for me.

❑ I'm afraid I'll disappoint someone if I tell them what I really want to do with my life.

If you relate to any of the above statements, read on for a few ideas about how to detour around this roadblock.

DETOUR  Determine whose opinion is most important.

Whose opinion about your life is important to you? Star the people who most influence your decisions.

❑ Family
- ❑ mom ❑ dad ❑ step-parent ❑ sister ❑ brother
- ❑ grandparent ❑ uncle ❑ aunt ❑ other family member_____

❑ Friends_____ _____ _____
❑ Best Friend _____
❑ Significant other
❑ Church
❑ Local community
❑ Society
❑ Teachers _____ _____ _____
❑ Famous people (something you have read, seen on TV)
❑ Group you belong to (sports team, drama club, student government, etc.) _____
❑ Neighbor

DETOUR Sort out what their "footsteps" look like.

You've heard the expression "following in someone's footsteps," right?

Often the important people in your life have their ideas about what your way should be or how it should look. This may even be based on the path or success of one person in particular. This idea may sound great, or it may not be your thing—for example, "Follow in my footsteps and become a doctor!" just may not feel true to who you are.

Or maybe you are being expected to avoid the path of someone who got in trouble or just didn't reach the level of success that was expected of him or her: "Don't follow in your brother's footsteps!" Or perhaps there is someone you admire and want to emulate: "I want to follow in her footsteps since she has such a great life." Or when a particular path seems too daunting: "Her shoes are too big to fill!"

So, who are the most important people in your life, and what do their footsteps look like?

Using the example, write down the most important people in your life, and their footsteps or "way." These people could be family, friends, teachers, neighbors, or even famous athletes, authors, actors, artists, politicians, or businesspeople whom you admire. Their footsteps could include career, family, education, opinions, financial status, or location. Underline any aspects that you want to be part of your own life.

Someone important to me	His or her footsteps
Example: My mom	Example: <u>Hardworking</u>, <u>strong</u>, <u>creative</u>, <u>self-sufficient</u>, <u>master's degree</u>, lives in a small town in the country, high school teacher, <u>well-respected</u>, tends to worry a lot.

 **DETOUR**   **Learn to be independent of others' opinions.**

> You must be independent of the opinion of others. No one can make you into what you are not. You are responsible to no one for your actions and thoughts except yourself. In addition, you are not in control of your reputation. All you can control is yourself and how you act on a day-to-day basis.
> —Dr. Wayne W. Dyer

Another person's opinion is just that: an opinion. It is not necessarily the truth or even in your best interest; it is just what that person thinks about a particular subject. You shouldn't place too much stock in anyone else's opinion, because everyone has one, they are all different, and they are all out of your control. If you ask ten people for their opinions about your new outfit, you are going to get a wide array of answers. Some will like it, some will hate it, and some will be indifferent. The same can be said about your reputation. What is a reputation but someone else's opinion of you? Some people may like you, some may hate you, and others probably don't give you much thought at all.

As soon as you try to change your opinions or actions in an attempt to please someone else or to fit in, another person may come along with yet another, completely different opinion. How do you change yourself in a way that will please them both? That's right—you can't. Multiply this example by the six billion people now living on this planet, and you'll see how impossible it is to please everyone.

This is not to say that you shouldn't consider the opinions of others, just that you shouldn't base your life on them, especially if it means sacrificing the values that make you who you really are. What really matters is what *you* think about yourself—something that is in your complete control. In the end, you, more than anyone else, know what's best for you. You were born with a natural intuition that will guide you in the direction that is best for you. All you have to do to feel good about yourself is decide to listen to your own guidance rather than following those around you.

 **ROAD BLOCK** #2: "I can't figure out what 'my way' is."

> You have your way. I have my way. As for the right way, the correct way, and the only way, it does not exist.
>
> —Friedrich Nietzsch

Do any of these describe you?

❑ I feel lost.
❑ I'm not sure what I really believe in.
❑ My parents have been telling me what to do for so long that I'm not sure what I really want to do.
❑ I don't know how to figure out what I really want to do.

❑ Sometimes I do things that don't represent "me."
❑ There are so many choices—how do I know which is the right one for me?

If you relate to any of the above statements, read on for a few ideas about how to detour around this roadblock.

 **DETOUR** ➤ | Sort out "my way" from "your way" on the little things.

You have spent most of your life influenced by someone else's "way." To get along in school, you learned your teacher's way. To get along at home, you learned your parents' way. To get along as a citizen of your community, you learned society's way. Learning these rules helped you avoid conflict and stay out of trouble, but spending too much time and effort trying to live by someone else's rules can make you lose sight of your way.

What separates your way from someone else's? Using the example below, write in some of the ways that you think or that you use to order your life that are different from another person's way.

Examples:
My mom thinks my music is just a bunch of noise.

My best friend likes to tell everyone her life story.

My teacher thinks everyone in our class should start college right away.

Examples:
I think punk music is inspiring.

I share my personal life only with people I'm really close to.

I'm not ready to go to college just yet—maybe in a couple years.

DETOUR ➤ Listen to your heart, to your intuition.

It's easy to separate your way from someone else's when only the small things are at stake, like your preference of music, how you dress, or the way you drink your coffee. But the bigger decisions can be tougher to make on your own when you have been influenced for so long by family, school, friends, and other outside sources. How do you determine what your way is? Whom or what do you listen to?

Most of us operate using a combination of "inputs":
1. **Information** and opinions we have absorbed from others.
2. **Lessons** we have learned from our past (experience or logic).
3. Our inner **feelings** about what's right (what our heart or emotions tell us).

Let's look at these in a little more depth:

#1: Outside opinions can be very valuable, but you must always take them with a grain of salt.

After all, no one else has had the experiences that have made you who you are; thus, they can never fully understand where you are coming from. The advice they offer can only be their interpretation of your way, or what they hope your way will be Sometimes it's tough for others to see you go through the process of figuring out your way, and so they make suggestions intended to make your life easier, even though it seems they are just telling you what to do.

#2: As hard as it is to believe, what your mind sees as logical may not be an accurate representation of your way, either. What you see and hear from others and the media greatly influences your understanding of the world and, therefore, your logic. Often your "logical" justification is just someone else's idea or opinion dressed up as your own.

#3: The most reliable guidance you have when it comes to figuring out your way comes from inside you. Call it what you will: your heart, gut, or feelings—in other words, **your intuition**.

DETOUR ➤ "Hell, yes!" versus "Hell, no!"

In his book *Why Your Life Sucks and What You Can Do about It*, Alan Cohen says that anytime you are presented with an idea or decision, you have an immediate internal reaction of "Hell, yes!" or "Hell, no!" A "Hell, yes!" response comes from an opportunity that gives you the feeling of freedom, empowerment, and excitement. This response comes when an idea is in line with your heart, your intuition, and your vision.

We react with a "Hell, no!" when an idea feels as though it limits our freedom, steals our enthusiasm, or is something that we really don't want to do. It may present itself as a feeling in the pit of your stomach or just as a lack of excitement. Sometimes it even comes up as an actual physical symptom. We're not just talking about taking out the garbage, or a responsibility that you have to fulfill to get through your everyday life—sometimes these tasks are necessary and we can't get out of them. Rather, we are talking about the decisions you make that shape the rest of your life—questions about career, education, where to live, and whom to spend your time with. Cohen says that if an idea is not a "Hell, yes," then it's a "Hell,

no"—at least for now. This is not to say that if you are presented with a similar situation again in the future, it will or won't be a "Hell, yes" then—it just isn't a match with where you are right now.

> *A "Hell, no!" response that we ignored:*
> *In 2003 we decided that we needed a change, so we gave a lot of our belongings away, put the rest into storage, and moved, sight unseen, from Seattle to the Big Island of Hawaii. We committed to working for a man on a small, isolated, solar-powered goat farm for one year! Upon arrival at our new home, our first impression was "Hell, no!" We knew right away that there was something about the situation that did not fit who we were, but our "logic" told us that since we had committed to being there a year, we should stay despite our discomfort. After a few months of this, we talked to the owner about our feelings, telling him that we thought we should leave early. To this, he told us that we were bad people, lacking in decency and integrity for even thinking about leaving before our year was up. Even our parents were begging us to get out of this situation because they could see that it didn't fit us. Finally, after six months of discomfort turning into anger, anger turning into depression, and depression nearly turning into despair, we decided to follow our hearts and leave early. This was the best decision we could have made. Doing so allowed us to move into a situation that was a better match for us, and allowed a new couple, who were a far better match for what the farm had to offer, to take our place.*

What's stopping you from living the life of your dreams?

DETOUR ➤ Practice "Right on!" and "You're serious?" responses.

Since you don't want to go around yelling "Hell, no!" to the people who care about you the most, we'll tone it down a little. You can keep that response inside, but how about trying "Right on!" for an idea that really resonates with you, and "You're serious?" for anything that doesn't thrill you. If it feels as though you need to approach the person's idea even more gently, we've added a third response: "I don't want to hurt your feelings, but. . ."

Take the top 6 people whose opinion most matters to you and fill in the way that they have hinted, emphasized, or demanded that you live your life. In other words, how they want you to live your life "their way". We're not trying to kick up a major rebellion in you, but help you sort out the advice that makes you excited to get out of bed in the morning and the advice that quite honestly doesn't. Living your life "your way" is not about rebellion. It is about living true to your heart and following your intuition.

Important person #1: _____
My Life Their way:_____
_____
_____
My immediate response:
❑ Right on!
❑ You're serious?
❑ I don't want to hurt your feelings, but . . .

Important person #2: _____
My Life Their Way:_____
_____
_____
My immediate response:
❑ Right on!
❑ You're serious?
❑ I don't want to hurt your feelings, but . . .

Important person #3: _____
My Life Their Way:_____
_____
_____
My immediate response:
❑ Right on!
❑ You're serious?
❑ I don't want to hurt your feelings, but . . .

Important person #4: _____
My Life Their Way:_____
_____
_____
My immediate response:
❑ Right on!
❑ You're serious?
❑ I don't want to hurt your feelings, but . . .

Important person #5: _____
My Life Their Way:_____
_____
_____
My immediate response:
❑ Right on!
❑ You're serious?
❑ I don't want to hurt your feelings, but . . .

Important person #6: _____
My Life Their Way:_____
_____
_____
My immediate response:
❑ Right on!
❑ You're serious?
❑ I don't want to hurt your feelings, but . . .

DETOUR ➤ Reality check on your parents' hopes, dreams, and expectations.

Are you afraid of what your parents expect of you, or afraid to tell them your dream? You may think you know what your parents expect of your life, but sometimes, if you actually ask them directly, you may get a different answer from the one you expected. Ask your parents what they expect from your life, and pay attention to your reactions to what they say. Was there anything they said that surprised you or that you would actually consider doing? This should give you some insight into your parents' *actual* hopes and dreams for you, not just your perception of them. You may decide to share some parts of the book, such as your life vision, with them to keep them in the loop. Many times you will find that your parents can support you in your ideas if they have a clue where you are going. It's usually when they don't have a clue that they start offering their opinion, in an attempt to help. Even if you decide to take your life in a different direction from the one they are suggesting, you will at least have had the opportunity to share your thoughts and ideas.

ROAD BLOCK #3: "But what if I fail?"

He who never makes mistakes, never makes anything,

—An English Proverb.

Do any of these describe you?

❑ I'm afraid of failing, so I'm not sure I want to try.

❑ To avoid failure, I'm planning to follow a safe and predictable career path.

❑ I'm afraid that someone I care about will say "I told you so" if I fail.

❑ What I really want to do is too risky.

❑ I don't want to be seen as a failure.

❑ I don't want to study a certain subject, because I might not be smart enough to succeed.

If you relate to any of the above statements, read on for a few ideas about how to detour around this roadblock.

DETOUR → Appreciate failure as a necessary part of the learning process.

The solutions to almost all life's problems are found by trial and error. You try something, and if it doesn't work, you try something else, repeating this process until you succeed. You may have been raised with a fear of failure, or at least a fear of being *seen* as a failure, which prevents you from trying in the first place.

One way of dealing with this fear of failure is to recognize that it is often from your worst failures that you learn the best lessons. It is with the experience incrementally gained from these failures that you can eventually create the success you are seeking. Here is what Thomas Edison said about his first ten thousand attempts to create a working electric lightbulb: "I have not failed. I have just found ten thousand ways that won't work."

This fear of failure also overlooks all the wonderful ways our society has benefited from discoveries that were initially considered mistakes. Cellophane, chocolate chip cookies, dynamite, ether anesthesia, fingerprinting, ice-cream cones, implantable pacemakers, matches, microwave ovens, penicillin, Post-It Notes, potato chips, sandwiches, Scotchgard, the Slinky, stainless steel, Teflon, and Velcro were all discovered by accident, many of them while attempting to solve a completely unrelated problem!

When you recognize the value in the lessons learned from mistakes made along the way, you will realize that failure is not to be feared but should instead be celebrated as a critical step in the process of achieving your dreams! Check out the exercise below.

Failures or Mistakes I've made:	What I learned/how it benefited me in the end:
Example: I nearly killed myself and my girlfriend because I was talking on my cell while driving.	Example: I got a headset for my phone, and I'm much more careful on the road. And it made me appreciate my relationship a lot more.

What's stopping you from living the life of your dreams?

What would you attempt to do if you knew you could not fail? —Unknown

R. Buckminster Fuller is a perfect example of someone who was able to conquer his limiting beliefs by making an agreement with himself to live his life as an experiment. At thirty-two, Bucky was so depressed about the state of his life that he was considering suicide. He had no money, no college degree, and had failed in every business venture he had attempted. Instead of killing himself, though, he decided to live the rest of his life as an experiment to see what one average man could do for the benefit of all of humanity. He even started referring to himself as Guinea Pig B! His experiment was a wonderful success, and he is now revered as one of the most revolutionary thinkers and inventors of the twentieth century.

Make a deal with yourself that will allow you to live a certain length of time as an experiment. If you can do this, the pressure to succeed will be greatly diminished, if not eliminated—after all, it's just a time of experimentation. If you succeed, great! Aren't you glad you went for it? If you "fail" or change your mind, you can come right back home and pick up where you left off, with no harm done.

Let's say you are thinking of moving to New York City to launch your acting career, but that little voice in your head kicks up, saying things like "There is no way you can succeed in the big city; you just aren't good enough." Or "The city is a dangerous place; you'd be safer just to stay home." This is when you make that deal with yourself: "I am going to live the next year of my life as an experiment. I will move to the city and attempt to launch my acting career. If, after a year, I haven't made appreciable progress toward my goal, I will move back home and resume my normal life. But if, after a year, I am having fun and enjoying even moderate success, I will give myself the option of continuing the experiment for another year."

If I had a year to live my life as an experiment here's what I would do:

> Death is not the biggest fear we have; our biggest fear is taking the risk to be alive—the risk to be alive and express what we really are.
>
> —don Miguel Ruiz

> Good people are good because they've come to wisdom through failure. We get very little wisdom from success, you know.
>
> —William Saroyan

ROAD BLOCK #4: "But what would happen if..."

> Don't be afraid to go out on a limb.
> That's where the fruit is.
>
> —H. Jackson Browne

Do any of these describe you?

❏ I have a big dream, but I'm afraid to pursue it, because there are so many "unknowns."

❏ I'm thinking about moving away from home, but I'm afraid of what would happen, whether I would like it, whether I would run out of money, or something worse.

❏ There is a career I'm thinking about, but my parents are worried about whether I would make enough money to keep afloat.

❏ I'd like to do some world travel, but I'm afraid of what might happen on the road.

❏ There's a subject I'm interested in studying, but I don't know how I would make a living with it.

If any of the above statements resonate for you, read on for a few ideas about how to detour around this roadblock.

 **DETOUR** — Recall other times when your fear turned out for the best.

Fear of the unknown often comes from your innate need for safety and security. There are parts of the mind that act as a personal alarm system designed to keep you out of danger. One of the ways the mind does this is to initiate a stress response in your body whenever you are in (or even just thinking about) an unfamiliar situation. Your stomach churns, your palms sweat, your hands shake, and your heart races, all in an attempt to encourage you back into the "safe zone." While there is comfort in what you know—what is safe and predictable—there are also fewer opportunities there for personal growth or new discoveries.

Have there been other times in your life when you were afraid of something but followed through anyway, and things turned out even better than expected? Sometimes remembering these experiences will give you that "Oh, yeah" response that can spark up the courage to try something new again. Even if you aren't convinced this will help you, do the exercise below.

Something I was afraid to do:	Why I'm glad I did it anyway:
Example: As a freshman, I really wanted to try out for the volleyball team but was afraid that I wouldn't be any good.	*Example: Not only did I make the team, I eventually became the MVP, and now I'm going to college on a volleyball scholarship!*

What's stopping you from living the life of your dreams?

DETOUR ➤ Confront your worst possible fear with reason.

Another way of confronting this fear of the un-known is to try to imagine the worst possible thing that could happen to you in a given situation, and then dismantle that fear by demonstrating how it will never come to pass. Marc Allen introduced this exercise in his "Millionaire Course" seminar, during which he said that his worst fear was of failing miserably in his business, ending up broke, living on the streets, and eventually dying in the gutter without anyone even noticing or caring that he was gone.

He was able to dispel this fear after really analyzing it and realizing that there was no possible way that he would ever let himself sink so low. There was always something that he, his family, or his friends could do to prevent the situation from getting that bad. He would take any job, move in with a friend, or accept government assistance—whatever it might take to keep him off the streets and get him back on his feet.

> A life spent making mistakes is not only more honorable but more useful than a life spent in doing nothing.
>
> —George Bernard Shaw

Take the time to spell out your worst fears in the left column below; then, in the right column, write a little about why those fears will never happen.

My worst fears	Steps I would take to keep this from happening:
Example: Ending up homeless, living on the streets because I lost all my money.	*Example: I would never end up homeless. I have a network of caring friends and family who would offer me a place to stay until I got back on my feet.*

DETOUR ➤ Rehearse a thought in your mind until it feels natural.

There is no use trying," said Alice…."One can't believe impossible things." "I daresay you haven't had much practice," said the Queen. "When I was your age, I always did it for half an hour a day. Why, sometimes I've believed as many as six impossible things before breakfast.
—Lewis Carroll, Alice in Wonderland

Everyone experiences times in life when they must leave their comfort zones to do something new or daunting. How do people such as professional athletes and stage performers, people who must perform at their best in front of thousands of people on a regular basis, quiet their personal alarm systems? The answer is practice, both physical and mental. The stage performer rehearses his material until he has mastered it. The athlete trains until she knows she can perform the feat required

of her. Both must also prepare mentally for these situations, picturing themselves on the stage or on the field, plying their skills in front of thousands of people, rehearsing the scenario in their minds over and over again until it feels "normal." When you have prepared this thoroughly for the situation, your alarm system is much less likely to blare out, demanding that you return to your comfort zone.

This technique works for just about any situation you could ever find yourself in, from public speaking and job interviews to asking that person you have been admiring from afar out on a date! Rehearsing your life vision statement would be a good place to start as you prepare to share your dreams with the people you care about.

ROAD BLOCK

#5: "I don't know how to make it happen."

> Go confidently in the direction of your dreams! Live the life you have imagined.
>
> —Henry David Thoreau

Do any of these describe you?

❑ I feel stuck.
❑ I just don't think I have any options.
❑ I'll never have enough money to do what I really want to do.
❑ I'm just not feeling very creative.

❑ I can't think "outside the box".
❑ I can't come up with any solutions different from those I've already tried.

If you relate to any of the above statements, read on for a few ideas about how to detour around this roadblock.

DETOUR ▷ Call on your friends for help.

Do you have a problem you just can't get around—are you having trouble "thinking outside the box"?

This is one of the reasons we have good friends, isn't it? Friends bring a fresh perspective to your situation because everyone sees things a little differently. Often a quick call, e-mail, or coffee break with a friend or two can get you on the right path quickly. For bigger issues, you might have to bring in even more help, which is where the "idea storm" comes in.

If you are feeling stuck or can't see around an obstacle in your way, find someone you trust to listen to your problem and give you some ideas. How would they solve your problem if they were in your shoes?

If it's a bigger quandary, one with far-reaching effects on your life in general, here's another way you can call on the help of your friends:

Ask a close friend these questions:
1. What do you see me doing in ten years?
2. What skills or talents do you think I have?
3. What do you think I can accomplish in my life?

Then, after your friend answers these questions, ask yourself, *What's my reaction to my friend's ideas?* If the answers your friend gave you made you feel good about yourself, then take some time to explore the possibilities of these new insights. If the friend's thoughts about your future didn't quite resonate with you, then express your appreciation but disregard that friend's words, and seek out the advice of another.

DETOUR ▷ Hold an Idea Storm party.

This exercise comes from Barbara Sher's book *I Could do Anything If I Only Knew What It Was*. It goes like this. Call up a group of friends and invite them to get together at your house. You start by giving everyone a quick overview of your situation before asking for their feedback. When everyone is up to speed with what you need, either designate a fast writer to take notes or get a voice recorder ready; then let the idea storm begin! Basically, you are going to pose a specific question about your situation, set a stopwatch for one minute, and then let the ideas fly! Each specific question gets one minute before you move on to the next one.

Say you want to take a gap year in Australia, and you need to leave soon, but you don't know how to

get everything done on time....
You say: "I don't have enough money to go . . ."
They say: "Visit your rich uncle," or "Sell your car," or "Get a summer job."

You say: "How do I sell my car fast?"
They say: "Put it on Craigslist on the web," or "Put a sign on it and park it at the gas station."

You say: "I don't speak Australian."
They say: "You're kidding, right?"

Some of the ideas that come out of this exercise are going to be a little strange, but it's very likely that someone will come up with exactly what you've been looking for.

What's stopping you from living the life of your dreams?

ROAD BLOCK

#6: "My thoughts are controlling me!"

> *Whether you think you can or think you can't, you're right.*
>
> —Henry Ford

Do any of these describe you?

❑ I feel as though I'm having a continuous argument in my head.
❑ I can't make up my mind about anything.
❑ I seem to doubt my abilities more than I believe in myself.
❑ I let little things people say get to me, and I replay them in my head.

❑ One voice tells me to go for my dreams, but the other tells me I can't do it.
❑ I make up stories about things not turning out right.
❑ I can't picture a happy ending to my life.
❑ I'm not good enough, smart enough or talented enough to pursue the life I really want.

If you relate to any of the above statements, read on for a few ideas about how to detour around this

DETOUR — **Use your Creative Mind rather than your Reactive Mind.**

So much of what you experience from day to day takes place only in your mind. If you can manage what is going on in your head, you will have more control over your life than you ever had before.

The character Socrates in the movie *Peaceful Warrior*, based on the book by Dan Millman, calls the mind a "reactive organ." When something good happens we react in one way, and when something bad happens we react in a different way. A reactive mind automatically goes into a programmed set of responses for certain situations. The opposite of the reactive mind is the creative mind. The creative mind responds to a situation by stopping to think about the reasons for the situation, rather than simply reacting to it.

Say someone cuts you off in traffic. You are seriously annoyed and immediately label that person a jerk. For the next few minutes you think about this experience and seethe. It seems logical at the time to react like this, but if you were to use your creative mind, you might find that there are a thousand other responses to this situation. Instead of instantly assuming that the person who cut you off is a

jerk, you could see the situation completely differently. Maybe the person didn't see you; maybe he just made a mistake and felt bad later; maybe he had an emergency. It doesn't matter whether any of these things are true—what is more important is how much you are willing to let this small event take over your mind and bring you down. **You can have a lot of power over your experience just by changing how you look at things.**

Imagine that you have been looking forward your whole life to going to a certain college, but for some reason you don't get in. You can look at this situation either as a tragedy, allowing it to bring your life to a grinding halt, or as an opportunity for something new, exciting, and unexpected to unfold in your life.

I didn't get into the college I wanted to. I can't believe it! I was totally counting on getting in. Now what am I going to do? Who else will even accept me? I'm such a loser.

There are many other colleges to choose from, and others who will accept me. Maybe that one wasn't going to be the best fit for me anyway. I have plenty of time to make another plan. It's not the end of the world.

Most of what we perceive as "reality" exists mainly in our heads. This includes every time you second-guess your actions and decisions, make up stories about what other people are thinking, or doubt your own skills and abilities. As Neale Donald Walsh says in *Home with God,* "Perspective creates perception, and perception creates experience."

To make this a little simpler, **how you look at something changes how you see it, and how you see things has a lot to do with how you experience them.**

If you see yourself as a loser, you may make decisions based on this low opinion of yourself. You may be less likely to try new things, because you may believe that you can't succeed. This thought begins as a very simple idea, but it can prevent you from living your dreams.

If, instead, you see yourself as being able to accomplish anything and as having the right to live a happy life, there is no stopping you!

DETOUR ➡ Map out your minutes.

> A happy person is not a person in a certain set of circumstances but rather a person with a certain set of attitudes.
>
> —Hugh Downs

But what happens when you seem unable to let go of a worry about something that is important to you?

Sometimes you have one of those nagging experiences that drives you crazy the more you think about it. Maybe you are really dreading something because you just KNOW that it will go horribly wrong. This is one of those times when your thoughts have control over you. You cannot think straight about a situation because you have already convinced yourself that no good outcome is possible. This calls for a serious change in thoughts.

In their book *Ask and It Is Given,* Esther and Jerry Hicks recommend a technique called "segment intending," which will help you create, rather than react to, your circumstances. The purpose of this technique is to prepare yourself mentally for each new segment of your day, imagining just how you would like the event to unfold before it even begins.

The idea behind it is simple: **you get out of a situation what you put into it and what you expect from it.**

An athlete who is confident in her abilities and can truly "see" herself winning the race stands a much greater chance of winning than someone who is unsure of herself and doesn't expect to win.

We call this process a **Minute Map**.

Just as you are using this book to map out your future, you can map out every day a little at a time. If you are nervous about something, take a few minutes the day before or even the morning of, and imagine what you want your day to look like. This will allow you to begin your day with excitement and anticipation of what is to come.

If you really can't believe the outcome that you are imagining, try instead just to relax, and appreciate something about the situation. This will usually lighten your mood enough to shift your thinking.

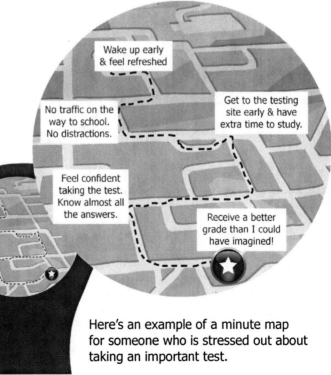

Wake up early & feel refreshed

No traffic on the way to school. No distractions.

Get to the testing site early & have extra time to study.

Feel confident taking the test. Know almost all the answers.

Receive a better grade than I could have imagined!

Here's an example of a minute map for someone who is stressed out about taking an important test.

Any other roadblocks that come up? Which detours would help you get around them?

Part 4

Putting It
all Together

My Dream List

Here's your chance to put it all together and create your Dream List.

1. List any visions that you have written.
2. Write out any goals related to your visions. There is space at the end for goals unrelated to any of your visions. If you need help, look back on John Goddard's Life List on pages 14 and 15. Some of these goals may be the same as your other missions or the steps to your vision.
3. Your dream list is a work in progress. You can add to this list at any time. You can cross things off or uncross ones you crossed off earlier. Check back on these lists from time to time to see if you're still on track. Change your visions if they have evolved.
4. Consider sharing your dream list with close friends or family members if you feel comfortable doing so. The people who care about you can best support you if they know what your vision is.
5. You can download additional copies of these pages from www.wheresthemap.com if you need them in the future.

Vision for My Education:
Page 44

❑ _____   ❑ _____

❑ _____   ❑ _____

❑ _____   ❑ _____

❑ _____   ❑ _____

❑ _____   ❑ _____

Vision for My Gap Year:
Page 61

❑ _____   ❑ _____

❑ _____   ❑ _____

❑ _____   ❑ _____

❑ _____   ❑ _____

❑ _____   ❑ _____

Vision for My Career:
Page 77

☐ _____   ☐ _____

☐ _____   ☐ _____

☐ _____   ☐ _____

☐ _____   ☐ _____

☐ _____   ☐ _____

Vision for My Place to Fit in:
Page 92

☐ _____   ☐ _____

☐ _____   ☐ _____

☐ _____   ☐ _____

☐ _____   ☐ _____

☐ _____   ☐ _____

**Vision for My Friendships,
Family and Relationships:**
Page 107

☐ _____   ☐ _____

☐ _____   ☐ _____

☐ _____   ☐ _____

☐ _____   ☐ _____

☐ _____   ☐ _____

My Dream List cont'd

Vision for What Keeps Me Going:
Page 118

- ☐ _____
- ☐ _____
- ☐ _____
- ☐ _____
- ☐ _____

- ☐ _____
- ☐ _____
- ☐ _____
- ☐ _____
- ☐ _____

Vision for Travel:
Page 125

- ☐ _____
- ☐ _____
- ☐ _____
- ☐ _____
- ☐ _____

- ☐ _____
- ☐ _____
- ☐ _____
- ☐ _____
- ☐ _____

Vision for My Spiritual Life:
Page 127

- ☐ _____
- ☐ _____
- ☐ _____
- ☐ _____
- ☐ _____

- ☐ _____
- ☐ _____
- ☐ _____
- ☐ _____
- ☐ _____

Now take a look at your life vision on page 31. After reading your visions for the other areas of your life, such as education, career, and relationships, is there anything about your life vision that you would like to change? Here is a chance to rewrite it:

My Life Vision:

Other Visions, Missions or Steps:

❑ _____   ❑ _____

❑ _____   ❑ _____

❑ _____   ❑ _____

❑ _____   ❑ _____

❑ _____   ❑ _____

❑ _____   ❑ _____

❑ _____   ❑ _____

❑ _____   ❑ _____

❑ _____   ❑ _____

❑ _____   ❑ _____

❑ _____   ❑ _____

❑ _____   ❑ _____

> Your ideas are valuable, and other people may be inspired to read what you have written for your life vision. You can read others' life visions, as well as submit and post your vision online at www.wheresthemap.com.

My New Life Map

Where are you going from here? You can come back to these pages later down the road, when you want to document any of the steps you have taken since finishing the book.

**Finished
Where's the Map?:**

The
adventure
continues...

Congratulations!

We are thrilled that you made it this far!

We hope that you have enjoyed this journey through **Where's the Map?** Most of all, we hope you have identified your most important values, clarified your vision, and created a dream list that you are looking forward to accomplishing. These are the steps that lead to creating the life of your dreams. Now the fun begins, as you put your vision into action.

If we have learned anything over the past few years, it's that change is inevitable and constant. Although the ideas you wrote in the exercises may no longer apply to the circumstances of your life in a year or two, the tools found here can be used again and again to help you redefine your vision and set new goals down the road. It is our wholehearted wish that this process of contemplation, clarification, and goal setting is something that you will use frequently as your dreams evolve.

We sincerely hope that this is just the beginning of our journey together, not the end. We intend to build a **Where's the Map?** community where you and others can come for guidance and support of your hopes and dreams. Please check out the next page to learn how you can participate. Visit our site for links and other resources that didn't fit in the book.

We leave you with a quote from John Goddard:
"Life is a daily miracle.... We live in the best time in human history, a time when with planning, preparation, and a little discipline, the ordinary person can do extraordinary things. Life is meant to be lived fully, deeply, optimistically, without hanging on to the baggage of the past, with no fear of the future, to live each day completely."

Don't forget to have fun along the way!

Aloha,
Beth and Jim

Seven Great Ways to Get Involved

1. Offer your "two cents"
If *Where's the Map?* was helpful to you, please submit a quote or review to us. Just a sentence or two is all we need. If there was something that you didn't like about the book that you think definitely needs to be changed in future editions, or if you have something that would be a good addition the second time around, please let us know.

Do you have examples from any of the exercises (values lists, missions, visions, strategies, steps) or stories that you would like to share? We are looking for submissions from our readers to share on our web site or in future editions of *Where's the Map? Create Your OWN Guide to Life after Graduation.*

2. Listen to "Your Life Your Way" Internet Radio
Do you or a friend have any stories that you want to share on the air? We'd love to hear about your unique vision because your story may inspire others. Call us for an interview.

3. Subscribe to "Your Life Your Way" E-zine
Do you have any questions that you need some advice about? Submit your questions on-line and get some great ideas, resources, and links in our monthly e-zine. You can register for this on our web site.

4. Attend a "Where's the Map?" Workshop
Coming soon to a town near you! We will be hosting workshops for high school and college students in vision creation, how to share your vision with those you love, how to plan a gap year, and how to create the lives of your dreams.

5. Enroll in one-on-one vision coaching
Need a little more help than what this book can offer? Maybe you have a big dream and you don't know where to start? Or maybe you don't have a clue what you want to do with your life and need some help figuring it out? Consider enrolling in one-on-one coaching with Beth, Jim, or one of our team members.

6. Apply for a Gap Year Scholarship
Multiple thousand dollar scholarships will be awarded to our readers between the ages of 18-25 who wish to participate in a gap year. Applications are due by August 1st of each year. See the web site for more details and to download your scholarship application. Looking for scholarships for college— we have links for these opportunities as well!

7. Fund-raising for high schools
Maybe you have already graduated, but have a younger sibling or a parent who is still involved at your high school. We are happy to offer a 50% discount to school groups who want to sell books as a fund-raiser. Sales could benefit school book stores, sports teams, theater, music, art, or academic programs, and could be sold at games, concerts and other events.

For more information about these programs visit:

www.WheresTheMap.com

You can contact us directly through the web site or in any of the following ways:

Inspiration Publications, Inc. PO Box 1004, Kamuela, HI 96743
808-430-3406 | Fax: 866-535-5167 | info@wheresthemap.com

Author Acknowledgments

Thank you to all the authors who provided great inspiration throughout our lives and whose ideas directly contributed to this book:

Wayne Dyer: "Independent of the opinion of others . . ."
Used in multiple books and presentations by Dr. Wayne Dyer
http://www.drwaynedyer.com/

Alan Cohen : "Hell Yes Versus Hell No"
Used in multiple books and presentations by Alan H. Cohen including *Why Your Life Sucks and What You Can Do About It*, © 2002 Alan H. Cohen
http://www.alancohen.com/

R. Buckminster Fuller: "Live your life as an experiment"
The work of R. Buckminster Fuller is being carried on by members of the Buckminster Fuller Institute.
www.bfi.org

Neale Donald Walsch: "Perspective creates perception..."
Home with God © 2006 by Neale Donald Walsch.
www.nealedonaldwalsch.com

Marc Allen: "My worst fears" Exercise
Ideas cited from the Millionaire Course
© 2003 by Marc Allen, Published by New World Library
http://www.marcallen.com/

Barbara Sher: "Idea Storm" Exercise
Found in *I Could Do Anything If I only Knew What it Was*
© Barbara Sher, 2004, Published by Bantam Doubleday Dell Publishing Group
http://www.barbarasher.com

Dan Millman: *"Reactive mind vs creative mind"*
Ideas adapted from Peaceful Warrior © 2006 Universal/Lionsgate
A film adaptation of The Way of the Peaceful Warrior
© 1980 Dan Millman, Published by New World Library Inc.
http://www.danmillman.com/

Jerry and Esther Hicks: "Segment Intending"
Found in Ask and It Is Given © Jerry and Esther Hicks, 2004,
Published by Hay House Inc.
www.abraham-hicks.com

John Goddard's teenage life list was used with permission from the author.
The Survivor: 24 Spine-Chilling Adventures on the Edge of Death
© 2001 John Goddard, Published by Health Communications Inc.
www.johngoddard.info

Also thanks to a few more authors whose inspiring words contributed indirectly to this book: Tom Brown Jr., Jack Canfield, Mark Victor Hansen, Nicholas Lore, Lisa Nichols, Daniel Quinn, and James Redfield.

QUICK ORDER FORM

Do you need another copy for a friend or relative? Here's how you can order more:

Fax orders: 866-535-5167 (Toll-free). Send this form.

Telephone orders: Call 808-430-3406 (Hawaii). Have your credit card ready.

E-mail orders: orders@wheresthemap.com

Web orders: Go to www.WheresTheMap.com and Click on the Gift Shop link.

Postal orders: Inspiration Publications, Inc., PO Box 1004, Kamuela HI 96743

I would like to order _____ copies of *Where's the Map? Create Your OWN Guide to Life after Graduation.*

Name: _____

Address: _____

City: _____ State: _____ Zip: _____

Telephone: _____

E-mail address: _____

Shipping: Please add $4.60 for the first book and $2.00 for each additional copy. Please call us for international shipping estimates.

ATTN: QUANTITY DISCOUNTS ARE AVAILABLE TO YOUR COMPANY, EDUCATIONAL INSTITUTION OR ORGANIZATION for reselling, educational purposes, subscription incentives, gifts or fundraising campaigns. If you would like to order more than 10 copies, please call our office for bulk discount rates, or visit our web site for more information.

Hey Parents!

Need some more help? Let's face it, being a parent isn't easy.

We've got some great resources for you too, whether your son or daughter is still in high school, has graduated, is attending college, or has "left the nest" completely.

Visit **www.WheresTheMap.com** for articles including:

- "Graduating beyond indecision: How you can help your son or daughter create a vision for the future."

- "Is your teen ready to go to college? How to figure this out, and what to do if it's just not the right time."

- "Why taking time off before hitting the books may be the best thing for your graduate"

- "How to support your grad's life vision."

Plus you'll find links to resources, web sites, and books that are great for parents.

Sign up for our **Parent's Way** newsletter for updates on coaching, teleseminars, and downloadable e-books and podcasts, plus other tips to help you best support your grad, and yourself.

Coming soon...

The parents' companion e-book

Where's My Map?
How You Can Help Your Kids
Create THEIR OWN Guide
to Life after Graduation

Printed in the United States
110371LV00003B/165-340/P